T0316565

Cambridge Elements ☰

Elements in Digital Literary Studies
edited by
Katherine Bode
Australian National University
Adam Hammond
University of Toronto
Gabriel Hankins
Clemson University

ACTUAL FICTIONS

Literary Representation and Character Network Analysis

Roel Smeets
Radboud University

CAMBRIDGE
UNIVERSITY PRESS

CAMBRIDGE
UNIVERSITY PRESS

University Printing House, Cambridge CB2 8BS, United Kingdom

One Liberty Plaza, 20th Floor, New York, NY 10006, USA

477 Williamstown Road, Port Melbourne, VIC 3207, Australia

314–321, 3rd Floor, Plot 3, Splendor Forum, Jasola District Centre,
New Delhi – 110025, India

103 Penang Road, #05–06/07, Visioncrest Commercial, Singapore 238467

Cambridge University Press is part of the University of Cambridge.

It furthers the University's mission by disseminating knowledge in the pursuit of
education, learning, and research at the highest international levels of excellence.

www.cambridge.org
Information on this title: www.cambridge.org/9781009180795
DOI: 10.1017/9781009180788

© Roel Smeets 2022

First published 2022

A catalogue record for this publication is available from the British Library.

ISBN 978-1-009-18079-5 Paperback
ISSN 2633-4399 (online)
ISSN 2633-4380 (print)

Actual Fictions

Literary Representation and Character Network Analysis

Elements in Digital Literary Studies

DOI: 10.1017/9781009180788
First published online: July 2022

Roel Smeets
Radboud University

Author for correspondence: Roel Smeets, roel.smeets@ru.nl

Abstract: This Element sheds new light on the ubiquitous yet complex notion of mimesis. By systematically comparing the social dynamics of the Dutch population at a given time with the social dynamics of characters in Dutch literary fiction published in the same period, it aims to pinpoint the ways and the extent to which literary fiction either mirrors or shapes the societal context from which it emerged. While close-reading-based scholarship on this topic has been limited to qualitative interpretations of allegedly exemplary works, the present study uses the data-driven tools of social network analysis to systematically determine the imitative elements of the social dynamics of characters within larger-scale, representative collections of books of literary fiction.

This Element also has a video abstract: www.cambridge.org/smeets

Keywords: Dutch literature, character network analysis, mimesis, digital humanities, social network analysis

ISBNs: 9781009180795 (PB), 9781009180788 (OC)
ISSNs: 2633-4399 (online), 2633-4380 (print)

Contents

1 Introduction

1.1 Literary Fiction and Social Reality

Where does fiction begin and reality end? While the myriad intersections of literature and society have traditionally been at the core of literary scholarship,[1] it is hard to draw clear-cut boundaries between stories and the social, historical, economic, and cultural environments in which they function and were created. It seems obvious to point out that literary fiction does not exclusively exist in the space between the front and back covers of a book. Not only are the fictional worlds depicted within its pages often modeled on the world "outside" the story, but they also have the potential to shape, influence, distort, or provoke the norms, values, customs, and beliefs of a time and a place. But although the boundaries between fiction and reality are evidently fluid and porous, one of the most foundational concepts of literary theory assumes a binary opposition between the two. From Plato onward, the term *mimesis* has invoked numerous juxtapositions between the two seemingly (in) separable domains of fiction and reality, literature and society, art and life.

This Element sheds new light on this ubiquitous yet complex notion of mimesis. By systematically comparing the social dynamics of the Dutch population at a given time with the social dynamics of characters in Dutch literary fiction published in the same period, it aims to pinpoint the ways in which, and the extent to which, literary fiction mirrors or shapes the societal context from which it emerged. While close-reading-based scholarship on this topic has been limited to qualitative interpretations of allegedly exemplary works, the present study uses data-driven tools of social network analysis to systematically assess the imitative elements of the social dynamics of characters within larger-scale, representative collections of books.

Showcasing some of the potential uses of social network analysis for the study of fictional worlds, this Element operates at the intersection between sociological and literary methods. In a benchmark article on the various forms that sociologies of literature have adopted in the past, James English (2010) has argued that the essence of sociological methods is *description*, whereas literary methods are often geared toward *critique*. The methodological claim of the present study is that social network analysis of literary characters contributes to

---

[1] Not only in the narrow sense of "symptomatic" forms of scholarship that considers literary texts as symptoms of deeper societal issues (cf. the discussion of this field in e.g. Felski 2015), but also in the broader sense of historicist approaches in which literature is studied in relation to its various – social, economic, cultural, and so on – historical contexts (e.g. Greenblatt 2005). Although some branches of literary studies have been famous for their text-centric approach (e.g. New Criticism or Russian formalism), it is safe to say that literature is only very rarely studied in complete isolation from the society in which it emerged or operates.

descriptions that can be used as a basis for close-reading-based critiques of fictional social dynamics. For discussions on mimesis and literature, a mixed-methods framework based on both description and critique is particularly useful. In order to pinpoint the complex relation between the fictional worlds of literary characters and the social reality of a society at a given time and place, this study uses social network analysis to describe statistically the encounters of characters in books and also uses the critical methods of cultural analysis to reflect on how these descriptions confirm or question theoretical claims on mimesis and literature. Whereas the statistical descriptions provided by social network analysis are necessary for systematic comparison between the social worlds of fictional characters and the social worlds of people, these descriptions evoke fundamental questions about the nature of literary fiction and its inter-sections with social reality that should be discussed with the critical tools of cultural analysis. Building on critical mimesis theory, this Element thus pays special attention to abstract, elusive notions such as "real," "fictional," and "reflection." What does it mean for a societal phenomenon to be reflected, mirrored, echoed, or reproduced in the dynamics between fictional characters?

Section 1.2 situates the present study within a long-standing discussion on the concept of mimesis. It does so by distinguishing between the two extremes in this debate: a reflection theory of mimesis stating that fiction *reflects* social reality and a control theory of anti-mimesis stating that fiction *shapes* social reality. While the various arguments for or against both theories have been expressed in unequivocal terms by proponents on both ends of the spectrum (respectively Plato and Oscar Wilde), the truth – as always – lies somewhere in the middle. It seems, furthermore, that most literary scholarship implicitly adheres to a more nuanced, gradual theory of mimesis in which literary works have the potential to both reflect and shape certain aspects of social reality up to a certain extent. I will use Caroline Levine's *Forms* (2015) as a theoretical vantage point from which to interpret the results of my analyses in light of this gradual spectrum. In Section 1.3, I will formulate the main research questions and hypotheses and outline the structure of the Element.

1.2 From Plato to Oscar Wilde: Mimesis versus Anti-mimesis

Mimesis is among the oldest and most fundamental concepts of literary theory. For that very reason it is particularly hard to outline its historical development without falling prey to a schematic representation of affairs.[2] Without any

---

[2] Trying to make sense of the "very long, and in many respects confused" history of imitation in literary theory, Colin Burrow contends that the concept of mimesis was "extremely complex in sense from its earliest recorded occurrences" (cited in Gregory 2020, 27).

intention of providing an all-encompassing overview of the various meanings the term has taken on throughout the ages, I briefly sketch the dynamic between Plato's earliest writings on mimesis and later Romantic attitudes toward the term.[3] This dynamic will serve as a theoretical point of departure that is unavoidably schematic but also provides a practical means to computationally operationalize questions about the ways in which literary fiction realistically reflects societal trends of a time and a place.

Since Plato's introduction of the term "mimesis" in the *Republic* it has continued to exert influence over theories of artistic representation. Derrida contended that "the whole history of the interpretation of the arts and letters has moved and been transformed within the diverse logical possibilities opened up by the concept of *mimesis*" (cited in Potolsky 2006, 2; emphasis in original text). At first glance, the idea that literature imitates life makes sense as authors often seem to write about the world around them. The history of literary theory has, however, witnessed a diverse range of attitudes toward this seemingly clear idea. While both Plato and Aristotle take their cue from the belief that art mirrors reality, they draw different conclusions as to the moral aspects of artistic representation. For Plato, the imitative nature of literature is a reason to ban poets and artists from the perfect city. As a mere copy of a copy ("twice removed from reality"), literature is illusory and deceptive. By contrast, Aristotle sees artistic imitation as perfectly "natural, rational and educational" and even "beneficial" (Potolsky 2006, 46). It does not merely copy the real; it has the potential to reveal universal truths and produce cathartic effects in human beings.

From Plato and Aristotle onward, writers, scholars, and critics from various disciplinary backgrounds have exploited the term for their own ends. The concept took on a life on its own far outside the realm of the arts and the humanities. In recent times, there has been an increasing interest in mimesis within both the social and natural sciences.[4] For the sake of clarity, I will stick to discussions on mimesis within the arts and the humanities – and more specifically to discussions on literary representation – without excluding the possibility that my findings are relevant outside the disciplinary boundaries of literary and cultural studies. Thus, while mimesis has been studied from a wide variety of research angles and fields (for an overview, see Gebauer & Wulf 1995; Potolsky 2006), this

---

[3] It is worthwhile noting that Plato discusses mimesis primarily in philosophical terms, while Romantic authors (like Oscar Wilde) did so primarily in terms of writing practices. Although the focus of these discussions is different (either scholarly or artistically), I will not make a fundamental distinction between the two because both types of discussions have equally shaped the intellectual discourse on mimesis.

[4] For an overarching, transdisciplinary view on mimesis, see the ERC-funded project Homo Mimeticus led by Nidesh Lawtoo at KU Leuven (www.homomimeticus.eu/).

Element narrows it down to mimesis in the sense of literary realism. To narrow it down even further, this Element does *not* address the mimetic processes of *imitatio* (how artists copy their role models) and theatre and theatricality (how audiences are influenced by art); instead it focuses specifically on the ways in which literature realistically depicts the world it was produced in.

The idea that literature reflects life, reality, or society in one way or another runs like a red thread through theories about literary representation from antiquity onward, although Plato's radical conclusion that literature therefore is deceptive and dangerous is only rarely repeated in later centuries. As of today, the seminal work of literary theory reflecting on this tradition is still Eric Auerbach's *Mimesis: The Representation of Reality in Western Literature* (1946 [2003]). Starting from the assumption that there is a relation between the rhetorical style of a literary work and the sociopolitical context of that time, Auerbach argues that each period in Western cultural history has its own particular way of "articulating reality" in literary form (2003; foreword by Said) by demonstrating this in works ranging from Homer's *Odyssey* (c. eighth century BC) to Virginia Woolf's *To the Lighthouse* (1927). Whereas Auerbach's study theorizes the relation between literary works and social reality explicitly in terms of mimesis, most modern literary scholarship assumes that there is such a relation – whatever form that may take – without emphasizing its particular dynamics.[5]

The conventional narrative states that theories arguing against the Platonic assumption that literature is a reflection of reality emerge mostly from the eighteenth and nineteenth centuries onward (e.g. Potolsky 2006). Famous in this respect is Oscar Wilde's anti-mimesis essay *The Decay of Lying* ([1889] 1891) for its *l'art pour l'art* claims that art only expresses its *own* contents and that life is not reflected in art but rather the other way around – that life imitates art. Wilde's theory is exemplary of the anti-mimesis paradigm shift within the Romantic period that was first described by M. H. Abrams in his seminal work *The Mirror and the Lamp: Romantic Theory and the Critical Tradition* (1953). The metaphor in the book's title serves to illustrate the rupture in literary history that allegedly took place in the Romantic period: whereas earlier writers tended

---

[5] Ideological approaches to literature, for instance, tend to assume that literary works are products of their environments without making explicit how the dynamics between literary fiction and social reality are manifested. A recent example is *Affectieve crisis; literair herstel* (2021; Affective crisis: Literary recovery) by Hans Demeyer and Sven Vitse, in which the authors analyze how millennial literature reflects, for instance, a particular response to present-day capitalist societies.

to view literature as a mirror of reality, Romantic writing was like a lamp illuminating the world and bringing color to gray social realities.

It seems safe to say that discussions on literary representation along the lines of Auerbach's and Abrams' seminal studies are prone to the classic "chicken or egg problem." Like most phenomena, literary representation as (anti-)mimetic is not an either/or issue but rather exists on a spectrum: it is fairly possible for a literary work to both reflect certain aspects of social reality and shape that same reality in other ways. For the field of Dutch literature, Jacob Jan Cremer's *Fabriekskinderen* (Factory children) (1863) exemplifies how literary works simultaneously reflect and shape social reality. Commissioned by a government official to help further legislation on child labor, the popular Dutch author visited a textile factory in the city of Leiden where children were put to work, after which he wrote an all-revealing novella that reflected the harsh realities these children were facing. This book is commonly regarded as having greatly influenced Dutch public opinion on child labor, which eventually resulted in legislation – the so-called "kinderwetje Van Houten" (1874) – that abolished labor for children below twelve years of age in the Netherlands. By means of a realistic literary depiction of children's working conditions, Cremer's book contributed to a shift in the societal debate on the issue. As such, *Fabriekskinderen* first reflected and then influenced social reality.

While Western literary history, at least since the upsurge of realism and naturalism, has witnessed a wide variety of other books that are known to have shaped social reality by realistically reflecting the (harsh) conditions of particular social groups,[6] the dynamic relation between fiction and reality for most literary works is probably not so crystal clear as it is in such examples. For the multitude of the less obvious cases, a tradition of literary criticism that prevailed between the 1930s and the 1950s seems particularly suited to grasping the gradual nature of (anti-)mimetic literary representations. Often working with relatively large corpora, these scholars systematically studied how societal trends (e.g. female employment, national norms and values, divorce) were reflected in literary fiction at a given time (e.g. Inglis 1938; Berelson & Salter 1946; Barnett & Gruen 1948; Albrecht 1956). In 1938, for example, Ruth A. Inglis wrote an article with the ambitious title "An Objective Approach to the Relationship between Fiction and Society," in which she quantitatively compares the increasing female employment in the late 1930s in America

---

[6] To name just a few of the most famous ones from the nineteenth century: Harriet Beecher Stowe's *Uncle Tom's Cabin* (1852) influenced political thought on slavery by depicting the harsh reality of slaves; and Gustav Flaubert's *Madame Bovary* (1856) and Leo Tolstoy's *Anna Karenina* (1878) shaped discourses on gender hierarchies by realistically describing the social position of women around the time of their publications.

with the employment of female characters in 420 American short stories over a period of thirty-five years. This is her methodological point of departure:

> First, the heroine is statistically a simple, tangible unit of measurement which is comparable to the members of the feminine population at large. Feminine attributes have been a focal point in social change of late. Socially, politically, and economically women have entered new fields of activity. Increasingly large numbers of women have left their homes to work in offices or factories. Meanwhile, what was happening to the heroines of fiction? What percentage of them were gainfully employed? If there was an increase since 1900, did it precede or follow the actual increase in employed women? An increase in the number of women gainfully occupied followed by an increased number of employed heroines would constitute substantial evidence for the reflection theory. If the order of events were reversed, it would support the control theory, even admitting there were other factors than literature involved in the actual social change. (Inglis 1938, 527)

Does literary fiction precede or follow societal trends? The present study aims to take this seemingly simple yet complex question to the next level by applying cutting-edge methods of social network analysis to fictional worlds of characters (e.g. Labatut & Bost 2019; Smeets 2021). Such data-driven, statistics-based techniques can help to formalize the approach to literary representation as suggested by Inglis and her contemporaries. Following the basics of its methodological framework, this Element explores the two general hypotheses that Inglis uses as her point of departure:

1. literature reflects societal trends (the reflection theory); and
2. literature shapes or incites societal trends (the social control theory).

Although these hypotheses are of course extremely schematic (it is not *either* reflection *or* control), they nonetheless serve as a means to gain insight as to where literary works should be plotted on the reflection–control spectrum.

   Unlike Inglis and others working in this tradition of literary study, however, I want to avoid the impression that this is an either/or issue. In the data-driven analysis presented in Section 1.3, I start by using the techniques of social network analysis to pinpoint where and how elements of both reflection and social control seem present in the dynamics between Dutch literary fiction and society. This is the phase of *description*, which James English (2010) considers characteristic for sociological methods (see Section 1.1). As a framework for this phase of the research, the binary logic of the reflection and control theories are perfectly suited, since the goal here is to indicate the extent to which fictional social networks converge with certain societal trends. The simple question that is central in this phase is: how (dis)similar are networks in fiction to real-world networks?

For the next phase of *critique*, however, this question falls short of capturing the subtle meanings of these observed (dis)similarities between fiction and society. What does it mean if networks of fictional characters differ from or correspond with networks of people? And what does it tell us about mimesis?

Caroline Levine's *Forms* (2015) provides a theoretical vantage point from which to make sense of such questions. Although she does not focus specifically on the concept of mimesis, her book's ambition is to move beyond the deadlock that seems to have been reached in discussions between formalist and historicist literary scholars. While it seems obvious that it is not solely the content of a work nor only its historical contexts that ascribe meaning to it, various approaches to the study of literature typically foreground one of these two aspects. While, for instance, historicist approaches such as Greenblatt's New Historicism emphasize how literary works are products of their environment, formalist approaches such as New Criticism discuss literature on its own terms. Theoretical discussions on mimesis are also about what comes first: the literary work (e.g. Wilde) or the environment it is part of (e.g. Plato). Levine's work serves as an inspiration to get out of this deadlock in three ways. First, she proposes a wider definition of the term "form" that also includes sociopolitical experience. Forms, in her view, are everywhere. Form is not restricted to the aesthetic content of cultural objects (e.g. narrative structure, themes, style); formal arrangements are also found in, for instance, workplaces, households, politics, social events, and so on. Second, no form is a priori dominant. While, for instance, historicizing Marxist approaches tend to regard sociopolitical mechanisms as a base structure organizing everything including artistic expressions, Levine does not assume that either the social or the aesthetic is the root cause for the other. Third, forms can travel across domains and collide in many ways. Forms like the gender binary, for instance, are present in a variety of domains, both social and aesthetic. And while their arrangement will be influenced by the specific contexts they are manifested in (e.g. gender binaries might be hierarchically organized differently in Dutch politics than in Dutch fiction), forms, at their essence, exist on their own terms.

In short, Levine's new formalism is a promising theoretical point of departure for a study on mimesis and fiction because it moves beyond the binary logic of reflection and control theories. As such, it provides a less schematic, more subtle terminology with which to make sense of the statistical results that will be presented in the next sections. In a practical sense, however, Levine's approach is rather vague when it comes to operationalization. Although her analyses of case studies are well-argued and thought-provoking, it is unclear how to transpose them to other examples. In order to provide a more clearly outlined technique that can be used to apply Levine's ideas in scholarly practice more broadly, this

Element uses statistics-based character network analysis to study the encounters, collisions, and clashes between both social and aesthetic forms.

1.3 Research Questions, Hypotheses, and Outline of the Element

The central focus of this Element is the formal arrangement of the network, more particularly social networks of both fictional characters and people. For the sake of convenience, it takes literary fiction published in the Dutch language as its research object (because I am a specialist in this field), but its approach could easily be transposed to other language areas.

In the remainder of this Element, I use the term "Dutch literature" broadly to refer to works of literature written in the Dutch language. Although the Dutch language area is not restricted to the Netherlands and Flanders,[7] the corpora analyzed in the next sections exclusively contain works from authors born or living in these geographical areas. In terms of its potential readership and number of publications, Dutch literature is one of the minor European literatures.[8] But while Dutch literature, like all literatures, has a history specific to its own social, cultural, and economic contexts, its development conforms to broader cultural trends.[9] Romanticism, for instance, emerged relatively late in Dutch literature compared to other European countries, but it has undoubtedly left its mark on the literary field.[10] Also, in the last two decades or so it has

---

[7] Dutch also has an official status in other constituent countries within the Kingdom of the Netherlands, such as Aruba, Curacao, and Sint Maarten, as well as in Suriname, which is a former colony.

[8] For a reflection on the status of Dutch literature in a broader transnational context, see Elke Brems, Theresia Feldmann, Orsolya Réthelyi, and Ton van Kalmthout (2020), "The transnational trajectories of Dutch literature as a minor literature: A view from world literature and translation studies," *Dutch Crossing* 44, no. 2: 125–135, DOI: 10.1080/03096564.2020.1747005.

[9] See the nine-volume series on Dutch literary history *Geschiedenis van de Nederlandse literatuur*, published between 2006 and 2017. See also Willem van den Berg and Piet Couttenier, *Alles is taal geworden: Geschiedenis van de Nederlandse literatuur, 1800–1900* (Amsterdam: Prometheus, 2009); Jacqueline Bel, *Bloed en rozen: Geschiedenis van de Nederlandse literatuur 1900–1945* (Amsterdam: Prometheus, 2018); Hugo Brems, *Altijd weer die vogels die nesten beginnen: Geschiedenis van de Nederlandse literatuur 1945–2005* (Amsterdam: Prometheus, 2013); Frits van Oostrom, *Stemmen op schrift: Geschiedenis van de Nederlandse literatuur vanaf het begin tot 1300* (Amsterdam: Prometheus, 2006); Frits van Oostrom, *Wereld in woorden: Geschiedenis van de Nederlandse literatuur 1300–1400* (Amsterdam: Prometheus, 2013); Herman Pleij, *Het gevleugelde woord: Geschiedenis van de Nederlandse literatuur 1400–1560* (Amsterdam: Prometheus, 2007); Karel Porteman and Mieke Smits-Veldt, *Een nieuw vaderland voor de muzen: Geschiedenis van de Nederlandse literatuur 1560–1700* (Amsterdam: Prometheus, 2008); Inger Leemans and Gert-Jan Johannes, *Worm en donder: Geschiedenis van de Nederlandse literatuur 1700–1800: de Republiek* (Amsterdam: Prometheus, 2013); and Tom Verschaffel, *De weg naar het binnenland: Geschiedenis van de Nederlandse literatuur 1700–1800: de Zuidelijke Nederlanden* (Amsterdam: Prometheus, 2016).

[10] See, for instance, Marita Mathijsen, *Nederlandse literatuur in de Romantiek* [Dutch Romantic literature] (Nijmegen: Van Tilt: 2004).

become commonplace to accuse Dutch writers of an inward focus and navel-gazing,[11] which, however, seems to be part of a more global cultural trend that foregrounds affectivity (Demeyer & Vitse 2020). While some of the findings presented in the next sections are thus specific to the Dutch literary field, there is no fundamental reason to assume that Dutch literature exists in isolation from other literatures. It would be, furthermore, worthwhile to test in further research whether similar results would be generated for literature from other language areas.

While "fiction" and "literature" tend to be used as umbrella terms in discussions on mimesis (see Section 1.2), they are broad categories that encompass a variety of media and genres with their own histories and institutional contexts. Without suggesting that other media and genres are less relevant, I will narrow down these categories to the medium of the novel and more particularly the genre of highbrow literary fiction. The reason for this is twofold. First of all, I focus on the novel because there are various scholars claiming that this medium has played a pivotal role in the development of modern societies. Perhaps most famously, Lynn Hunt has argued in *Inventing Human Rights* (2007) that novels such as Jean-Jacques Rousseau's *Julie, ou la nouvelle Héloïse* (1761) have been crucial for the emergence of human rights because of their appeal to the reader's empathy. Others have put forward similar arguments about the historical function of the novel in modern societies.[12] In order to assess the dynamics between aesthetic and social form, the present study takes these theories as a vantage point for an empirical comparison of novels to their sociohistorical contexts. Second, as such theories tend to rely on a range of canonical, highbrow authors such as Jean-Jacques Rousseau and Harriet Beecher Stowe, I will equally focus on novels within the category of highbrow literary fiction. While being fully aware of the potential differences between low-, middle-, and highbrow forms of fiction,[13] the present study targets novels that are traditionally held in higher esteem than other forms of literary fiction for the very reason

---

[11] For a reflection on this accusation, see Saskia Pieterse, "Het hoogopgeleide navelstaren [The higher-educated navelgazer]," *De Groene Amsterdammer* October 31, 2018 (www.groene.nl/ artikel/het-hoogopgeleide-navelstaren).

[12] Ian Watt, for instance, emphasizes in *The Rise of the Novel* (1960) how the novel contributed to the changing societal position of women. And in a similar vein as Lynn Hunt (2007), Martha Nussbaum (2010), and Bas Heijne (2011) foreground the ways in which novels strengthen our empathy and moral involvement.

[13] In "The culture industry: Enlightenment as mass deception" (1947/2017), Horkheimer and Adorno famously conceptualized the division between "popular" or lowbrow and "literary" or highbrow forms of fiction by stressing their different social dimensions. In discussions about the middlebrow in Dutch literary fiction, it is argued that works in this category have a different relation to societal trends than do other types of fiction (e.g. Van Boven 2011).

that these are often the examples on which literary theory is based. The analyses in the next sections should be seen as a first step toward a systematic comparison of literary fiction and social reality – the goal is to carry out cross-genre and more extensive cross-period analyses on the same topic. Furthermore, there is a pragmatic reason to narrow down this Element's scope to one medium (the novel) and to one genre (highbrow literary fiction). As it is particularly hard to distinguish between genres computationally,[14] it was convenient that I could rely on an external criterion for the compilation of the Libris 2013 corpus (analyzed in Sections 2 and 3). All 170 novels in that corpus were submitted to the bulk list of the most prestigious literary prize in the Dutch language area and therefore made an appeal to the highest literary recognition possible. And although these kinds of literary prizes did not exist in the 1960s, I made an effort to compile a comparable collection of texts for the Sanders 1960s corpus (analyzed in Section 3). More information on the corpus collection and data extraction will follow in the methodological frameworks of the next sections.

The Element is divided into two complementary parts, the first of which takes a synchronic approach, focusing on one year of literary production, and the second a comparative approach, studying the changes between two periods of literary production. Here I will briefly introduce the research questions and hypotheses that will be assessed in the next two sections.

1. How similar are social networks of fictional characters to social networks of people at a given time and place?

In Section 2, I will compare a sample of network data from the Dutch population with a sample of character network data from Dutch literary fiction in the same period. Before doing so, I will first describe various computational techniques that can be used to extract character networks from literary texts and provide some arguments for the technique I developed earlier (Smeets 2021). Afterward, I will use this technique to compare social networks of 1,069 people within contemporary Dutch society with social networks of 2,137 characters in 170 literary novels written in the Dutch language. Two representative samples of data are used for this comparison that have been used in previous sociological and literary studies: the Survey of the Social Networks of the Dutch (SSND) and a heavily annotated collection of metadata on all identified characters in the Libris 2013 corpus (e.g. van der Deijl et al. 2016; Volker & Smeets 2019; Smeets 2021).

---

[14] See, for instance, Ted Underwood, "The life cycles of genres," *Cultural Analytics,* May 23, 2016. DOI: 10.22148/16.005.

Inspired by the two extremes to the debate on mimesis, I will take the following two hypotheses as points of departure:

1. character networks *reflect* dynamics within social networks of people and thus are relatively similar; and
2. character networks and social networks of people are dissimilar, possibly because the first *co-shapes* the second.

To narrow down the question, I will focus on one crucial aspect of social networks: segregation. How do divides along the lines of gender, ethnicity, education, and age within social networks of characters compare to actual social networks? This question is answered by interpreting the findings of a range of statistical tests in terms of mimesis and Levine's new formalist framework (see Section 1.2).

2. To what extent is the emancipation of women reflected in or shaped by the network position of female characters?

Whereas the previous research question is synchronic, focusing on one particular period of Dutch literary history, this question aims to track changes within two distinct periods: the 1960s and the 2010s. As a case study, it focuses on the ways in which one particular sociopolitical development converges with the structure of character networks. Given the changing position of women in society due to the emancipatory movements of second- and third-wave feminism, it explores the extent to which the position of female characters transforms in a period of approximately fifty years. While being critical of the linear historical narrative that the societal positions of women have increasingly improved between the 1960s and the present, Section 3 tests the hypothesis that female characters increasingly become more important in terms of network centrality. Whereas the previous research question builds on two ready-to-use datasets, a new corpus of Dutch fiction is warranted for this section. In order to compare how character networks have evolved over time, my student assistants and I have created a new corpus with 155 books of early 1960s Dutch literary fiction.

Both sections are grounded in the approach to character network analysis as presented in my book *Character Constellations* (2021). Based on the co-occurrence of characters on the sentence level (Smeets et al. 2019), it semi-automatically extracts social networks of fictional characters from contemporary literary texts written in the Dutch language.[15] This method for extracting character networks allows for an exploration of the two research questions in light of the long-standing discussion on mimesis and realistic literary representation.

---

[15] See https://github.com/roelsmeets/character-networks for all code and data.

The overall structure of the Element is as follows. Whereas Sections 2 and 3 zoom in on case studies that exemplify one aspect of the mimesis debate (segregation in Section 2, women's emancipation in Section 3), the final, concluding Section 4 zooms out again and connects these findings to the broader mimesis debate. Methodologically, these case studies serve as examples of how to apply computational and statistical techniques such as character network analysis to a long-standing theoretical discussion with regards to a core concept of literary theory. The goal of this Element, in other words, is thus not only to enrich our understanding of mimesis and literary realism but also to get literary scholars and students acquainted with the potential uses and challenges of social network analysis. In order to achieve that goal, I have tried to make this Element accessible to a nontechnical audience by clarifying some of the basics of computational techniques and statistical analysis while avoiding unnecessary terminology.

2 Novel Divides: Characters and People

This section explores the question how similar social networks of fictional characters in Dutch novels are to social networks within the Dutch population at a given time. It does so by focusing on one of the key challenges of present-day societies: segregation (e.g Briggs 2001). Social divides along the lines of cultural background, education, age, and gender are studied in both networks of characters and networks of people. One of the main findings of this section is that while segregation by cultural background seems high in Dutch literary fiction, it is relatively low compared to the Dutch population.

These results demonstrate how character network analysis can shed a new light on the ways in which literature realistically reflects the dynamics of the society in which it was published. In Section 2.1, some core assumptions of social network analysis are described, as is its application to fictional worlds of characters. Section 2.2 reports on the methodological set-up of the analysis and interprets the findings in light of discussions on mimesis and literary realism.

2.1 Character Network Analysis: Premises, Methods, Techniques

While there are various versions of the origin story of social network analysis,[16] most modern-day – often computer-assisted – uses rely on the application of graph theory to social worlds. As a mathematical discipline, graph theory is

---

[16] For an overview of some of these versions, see Linton Freeman's *The Development of Social Network Analysis* (2004). Whereas pioneers of classical sociology such as Georg Simmel and Emile Durkheim are often mentioned as forerunners of modern-day social network analysis, it is only since the 1930s onwards that more systematic research into social networks started to emerge.

designed to describe relations between objects, which are commonly called "graphs" or "networks" (hereafter, I will use the term "networks"). In its most basic form, a network consists of objects commonly called "nodes" and relations between these objects, commonly called "edges."[17] Applications of graph theory in the social sciences often target networks consisting of people as nodes and different types of relations between people as edges. Famous examples of studies using social network analysis include Stanley Milgram's small-world experiment (1967), in which he demonstrated that the average distance between people in the United States is only five or six people (often called "six degrees of separation"), as well as Mark Granovetter's "The strength of weak ties" (1973), which makes the case that "weak relations" such as acquaintances significantly impact social cohesion.

Taking their cue from insights in the field of social network analysis, literary scholars in the 2000s and 2010s have increasingly started to transpose these methods and techniques to the analysis of fictional worlds (e.g. Alberich, Miro-Julia & Rossello 2002; Stiller et al. 2003; Elson, Dames & McKeown 2010; Lee & Yeung 2012; Moretti 2011; Jayannavar Agarwal, Ju & Rambow 2015; Lee & Wong 2016; Grayson, Wade, Meaney & Greene 2016; Smeets 2021). But although it might seem just a small step from networks of people to networks of fictional characters, the phenomenon of character network analysis has brought along various practical and theoretical issues.

In a study on the social dynamics of characters in Shakespeare's *Hamlet*, Franco Moretti (2011; 2013) was one of the first to demonstrate the affordances and challenges of character network analysis. His contribution to the development of character network analysis as a tool for literary analysis has primarily been not on a practical-technical level (his work is technically fairly straightforward) but rather in terms of theoretical reflection. The main advantage of studying narratives in terms of character networks is that it enables a view of plot as "time turned into space" (2011, 3). Visualizing characters as nodes and their interactions as edges helps to transcend the boundaries of linearity that any qualitative assessment of texts is often confined to. Instead of going back and forth between pages, we can zoom out and focus on narrative progression in a nonlinear way, which Moretti describes as "making the past just as visible as the present" (4). Just as sociologists do not necessarily have to follow their respondents from birth to death in order to study their social interactions, character network analysis allows literary scholars to study the social dynamics between characters in a holistic way without having to read every single scene

---

[17] Depending on the specific application of graph theory (for instance, in social sciences, biology, physics, computer science), different terms are used to refer to nodes and edges. Nodes are also called "vertices" or "points." Edges are also called "ties," "links," or "lines."

where characters interact. Among other things, this enables scholars to describe power dynamics between characters quantitatively. How is the network structure of *Hamlet* affected, for instance, if you remove Hamlet or Claudius?[18]

Character networks such as these are models;[19] and the affordance of working with such models is that they "[allow] you to see the underlying structures of a complex object" (2011, 4). Indeed, the visualizations of these character networks allow one to relatively quickly get a sense of what the power distributions in Shakespeare's play – "the underlying structures" – look like (e.g. the networks fall more dramatically apart when Hamlet and Horatio are removed as opposed to when only Claudius or Hamlet are removed).

But literary texts are 'complex objects' and it is not an obvious task to use character network analysis to arrive at models that convincingly describe their 'underlying structures'. Part of the difficulty has to do with the central unit of character networks: characters. Although they share similarities, characters are different kinds of entities than people of flesh and blood. While there seems little room for disagreement about Toril Moi's proposition to study both the human-like and the text-like qualities of characters (and not impose an a priori taboo on treating characters as if they were real people),[20] it is nonetheless impossible to study social dynamics between characters the same way as sociologists study social dynamics in a population. To name only a few challenges: which characters do we count as nodes? Which types of interactions do we count as edges? How do we define the weight of the interactions?

In a sense, Moretti's analysis of *Hamlet* is a case of low-hanging fruit; character network analysis as a technique has moved past this particular application, especially by reaping the benefits of automated, computational analysis.[21] Theatre scripts tend to be structured in a uniform way, with straightforward building blocks for character networks: all names in the list of dramatis

---

[18]　See Moretti (2011).

[19]　In *Distant Horizons* (2019), Ted Underwood defines a model as "a relationship between variables" (xii). Perhaps ironically in light of Moretti's emphasis on models in this study, Underwood suggests that the turn toward modeling and hypothesis testing in more recent forms of digital literary studies is a move away from Moretti's earlier distant reading studies: "Instead of measuring things, finding patterns, and then finally asking what they mean, we need to start with an interpretive hypothesis (a 'meaning' to investigate) and invent a way to test it" (Underwood 2019, 17).

[20]　According to Toril Moi, this taboo is a consequence of the "modernist-formalist assumption that [character criticism] always presupposes a naive realism" and "rests on no sound philosophical grounds" (2019, 61–62). In her view, it is fully possible to study both the textual qualities and the person-like qualities of characters because 'texts are never just forms but also expressions, actions, and interventions' (67).

[21]　Examples of more advanced forms of character network analysis include Alberich, Miro-Julia, and Rossello (2002); Stiller et al. (2003); Elson, Dames, and McKeown (2010); Lee and Yeung (2012); Jayannavar Agarwal, Ju, and Rambow (2015); Lee and Wong (2016); Grayson, Wade, Meaney, and Greene (2016); and Smeets (2021).

personae can be taken as nodes, and edges between characters can be established when one of these names appears in the lines spoken by a character (e.g. "KING CLAUDIUS: How fares our cousin Hamlet?"). And although Moretti does not ascribe weights to the edges, one can easily define the weight of character interactions by the occurrences of a character name in the lines spoken by another character – a strategy that has been adopted by more recent character network analyses of dramatic plays (e.g. Karsdorp et al. 2015).

This approach would not work for texts in other genres, such as modern novels. Whereas the dramatis personae in a play intended to be performed on stage arguably contain all relevant characters of its fictional social world, novels lack an overview of its most important characters. Of course, one could take all person-like entities in a text that occur once or more (including every passenger, bus driver, window cleaner, et cetera), but this would result in a list of nodes consisting of a few main characters and a huge amount of minor and side characters – or, to speak in terms of Zipf's law, a small peak and an extremely long tail.[22] Sociologists would not even ponder the possibility of conducting social network analysis of each and every person within a population; instead they work with a representative sample of that population.

What, then, is a representative list of characters in a fictional social world? An answer to this question requires a fundamental reflection on, and perhaps reconsideration of, the narrative category of "character." While literary theory has produced a wide variety of definitions of "character," each emphasizing different aspects,[23] a most basic definition would be in line with what Fotis Jannidis in *The Living Handbook of Narratology* calls "a text- or media-based figure in a storyworld, usually human or human-like" (Jannidis 2013). However, in order to (semi)automatically extract character networks from literary texts, this definition is too abstract. A computer-assisted operationalization of this definition – often called "character detection" – requires defining measurable features of characters, such as their name and other linguistic

---

[22] In the field of quantitative corpus linguistics, Zipf's law was formulated to describe the phenomenon that the frequency of a word in a corpus of texts written in any natural language is inversely proportional to its position in the frequency rankings of all the words in the corpus. For instance, the most frequent word in a corpus of English (e.g. "the") occurs twice as often as the second most frequent word (e.g. "of") and thrice as often as the third most frequent word (e.g. "and"). This results in a small peak of relatively frequent words and a long tail of words that occur less often or only once. Our preliminary experiments suggest that something similar seems to hold for characters and their names.

[23] In the field of character studies, the ontological status of characters – where do characters exist, only inside or also outside the narrative (Reicher 2010)? – have resulted in different definitions. Other definitions stress the cognitive aspect and discuss the extent to which characters exist in the minds of the reader (Culpeper 2000), while John Frow (2014, 25) more broadly discusses the dilemma whether characters are "pieces of writing," "person-like entities," or a hybrid of those definitions.

referents. Representative sampling of characters in a fictional world, further-more, calls for a threshold such as: only take entities into account whose names occur at least an N amount of times, where N is relative to, for instance, the length of the text.

The next challenge is to come up with a formal definition of "relations" or "interactions" between characters on which the extraction of the edges in the character network would be based. Roughly speaking, there are two main strat-egies for this. The first – and this one is used in the Hamlet network – is to frame connections between characters in terms of conversations or dialogue.[24] For a dramatic play, this seems appropriate: its text is already structured as one extended or several shorter conversation(s) between different speakers, and the dynamics between the characters on stage take shape within the framework of such conversation(s). But although this strategy can also be adopted for other genres, such as novels, the lack of uniform structure (such as conversation-structured dramatic plays) make it particularly difficult. Indeed, some novels structure their conversations in a relatively uniform way (apostrophes, verbs such as "said" and "asked," question marks, and so on), but this is not a general rule, and other writers use different conventions (no apostrophes, for instance).

There is, furthermore, a theoretical problem with extracting edges in novels based on conversations: it narrows down the scope of character interactions considerably. While characters talking to one another can reasonably be expected to have an interaction, characters do not *only* interact through conver-sation or dialogue. Sometimes characters engage with one another by means of the simple fact that they occur in the same sentence, paragraph, or chapter. Compare this with social networks of people: a sociologist would probably not object to assuming a relationship between people in the same workplace who have not been in any conversation whatsoever. Admittedly, the bond between coworkers who never had a conversation is probably less strong than coworkers who talk constantly, but nonconversing coworkers are still part of the same social network for which their workplace provides the context. Not only does this shared context of the organization or office provide a general framework for social networks in the workplace, but it also opens up meeting opportunities for any two people working for the same employer.

For literary fiction, this broader definition of edges is often operationalized by framing connections between characters in terms of co-occurrences in the same window of N words, sentences, paragraphs, or chapters.[25] The rationale behind

[24] Elson, Dames, and McKeown (2010); Jayannavar, Agarwal, Ju, and Rambow (2015); Lee and Yeung, (2012); Lee and Wong (2016); Moretti (2013); Stiller et al. (2003).

[25] Alberich, Miro-Julia, and Rossello (2002); Grayson, Wade, Meaney, and Greene (2016); Smeets et al. (2019); Kraicer and Piper (2019); Smeets (2021).

this strategy is that characters who occur near one another in the text have greater meeting opportunities than characters who are separated by more words, sentences, paragraphs, or chapters. These meeting opportunities for characters, however, are different from the meeting opportunities between people. Unlike people, characters do not necessarily have to be part of the same thematic context (e.g. a workplace, a family, a circle of friends, a neighborhood) in order to be connected. Although characters who do share such a context are possibly more strongly connected than characters who do not, being linguistically adjacent to one another – co-occurring – also shapes connections between characters. As a reader, you would probably be inclined to associate characters with one another not only when they are friends, lovers, enemies, and so on but also when they are mentioned regularly in the same sentence.

The findings presented in the following section are the result of a character network analysis on a corpus of present-day Dutch novels that is based on the theoretical assumptions thus outlined. This is, however, not to say that other approaches to character network analysis are invalid. While other studies define nodes more inclusively as all or most human-like entities in a text (e.g. Kraicer & Piper 2019), my approach is restricted to characters who appear at least N times in the text, where N is relative to the length of the text. And while there are many good reasons to define edges in terms of conversations (for instance, when working on dramatic plays), my focus on present-day novels more naturally allows for a definition of edges in terms of co-occurrences for the reasons just listed.[26]

2.2 Character Networks Compared to Social Networks of People

How similar are social networks of fictional characters to social networks of people? This section compares character networks in Dutch novels with social networks within the Dutch population in a given time period. By doing so, it aims to shed light on the ways in which literary fiction realistically depicts one particular aspect of the social reality in which it was written and published. Inspired by studies on the imitative dimension of literary fiction published in the 1930s, 1940s, and 1950s (e.g. Inglis 1938; Berelson & Salter 1946; Barnett & Gruen 1948; Albrecht 1956), I will use this comparison between social networks of characters and people to assess the complex dynamics between the reflection and social control theories. This is, however, not a matter of straightforward hypothesis testing as one would encounter in sociological studies into

---

[26] In my case, these co-occurrences are defined in windows of two sentences. For an extensive elaboration on the most appropriate window unit (words, sentences, paragraphs, chapters) and window size, as well as a range of experiments I conducted to find the best approach, see Smeets et al. (2019) and Smeets (2021).

social networks of people. Although the following comparative analysis will make use of similar statistical techniques, its results do not suffice to simply reject or confirm a null hypothesis. As described in Section 1, there are no binary answers to the question how mimesis works for literature: it is not as if *either* the reflection theory *or* the social control theory holds true. Rather, the similarities and differences between character networks and networks of people will help to gain insights into the gradual aspect of (anti-)mimetic literary representation.

2.2.1 Corpus and Dataset

This section builds on some findings from my earlier work as well as on some results of joint work with sociologist Beate Volker (Volker & Smeets 2019). In *Character Constellations: Representations of Social Groups in Present-Day Dutch Literary Fiction* (Smeets 2021), I developed a theoretical and methodological framework to study literary representations of social groups in terms of network theory. Although I could have worked with literature written in any language and from any time period, my roots in contemporary Dutch literature led me to compile a corpus of all 170 novels submitted to one year (2012) of the most prestigious literary prize in the Dutch language area, the Libris Literatuurprijs 2013.[27] In terms of representative sampling, this corpus represents 37 percent of the literary novels originally published in the Dutch language in one random sample year in the 2010s (in this case, 2012), excluding nonfiction and other book genres, translations, and reprints.

Based on the co-occurrence of characters at the sentence level (Smeets et al. 2019), I developed a technique to semiautomatically extract social networks of the fictional characters from each of the novels in the corpus.[28] This approach is semiautomatic in the sense that it uses automatic named entity recognition to detect characters and their name variants ("Frits," "Frits van Egters," "Van Egters"),[29] after which errors are manually corrected for each individual novel. Following the arguments about character occurrence and Zipf's law from Section 2.1, only the N most frequently occurring characters were taken into account, resulting in an average of 13 detected characters per novel and a total of 2137 characters for the corpus as a whole. Each of these detected characters were then defined as nodes in a character network. Furthermore, manual annotation was conducted to define

---

[27] This prize targets books written in the previous year, which is why the submitted novels to the bulk list of the Libris Prize 2013 contains novels from 2012. For more information on the corpus, see Smeets (2021).

[28] See https://github.com/roelsmeets/character-networks for all code and data.

[29] For a reflection on the choice for coreference resolution based on only name variants, see Smeets et al. (2019).

a range of demographic metadata for each of these characters, if known: gender, country of origin, educational level, age, profession.[30] Edges between these nodes were automatically established when any two characters co-occurred in the same window of two sentences.[31] The weight of these edges were based on the *number* of co-occurrences; characters are considered more strongly connected in the character network when they co-occur more often. These 170 extracted character networks can then be used to test a range of hypotheses with regards to the centrality, communities, and conflicts of male versus female characters, characters with and without a migration background, higher- and lower-educated characters, and older and younger characters.

2.2.2 Comparative Network Analysis: Characters versus People

While I was conducting preliminary experiments with character network analysis, sociologist Beate Volker and I ventured into a collaborative research project that is still ongoing at the time of writing (March 2022). Both of us were fascinated by the question of how fictional worlds relate to their cultural and societal contexts. Narrowing down this extremely large question to an operationalizable case study, we decided to first focus on segregation. As it is a topic of primary concern in the sociological study of (in)equality (e.g. Briggs 2001; Cheng & Volker 2016), we set out to study the similarities and differences of segregation by descent, age, education, and gender in social networks of the Dutch population versus character networks in Dutch literature from the same time period. I will now report on some of our findings.

Collaborating with a sociologist helped me identify some methodological inconsistencies in my own work. While I earlier used corpus-based statistical patterns as a baseline to compare individual works against, these statistical patterns themselves lacked a baseline. Let me illustrate this. In order to get a sense of how segregated the character networks in the corpus were with regards to gender, descent, education, and age, I calculated so-called "assortativity" (also called "homophily") for each of these four variables. Ranging from −1 to 1, the assortativity coefficients represent the extent to which a character network contains connections between any two characters with the same gender, descent, education, or age. For instance, if a novel in the corpus has a gender assortativity coefficient of 1, then this novel only features same-sex relations (man–man, woman–woman) whereas a score of −1 means that this novel contains only opposite-sex relations (man–woman, woman–man). Thus, a gender assortativity of 1 means that the

---

[30] For more information on the data collection in the various research stages, see Smeets (2021).
[31] For an elaboration on experiments with different window units and sizes, see Smeets (2021).

character network is fully segregated by gender because no relations between characters of the opposite sex occur.

Computing assortativity coefficients for gender, descent, education, and age in each of the character networks extracted from each of the 170 novels in the corpus thus results in four scores ranging from −1 to 1 representing the amount of segregation by, respectively, gender, descent, education, and age for each individual novel. The novel *De lichtekooi van Loven* (2012) by Ineke van der Aa, for instance, has a gender assortativity coefficient of −0.05. As this score is close to 0 (on a scale from −1 to 1), this suggests that gender segregation and integration are relatively balanced in this novel: same-sex (man–man, woman–woman) and opposite-sex (man–woman, woman–man) relations occur almost equally often. These scores for individual novels are, however, meaningless if not compared to a statistical baseline. If most novels in the corpus have a gender assortativity coefficient near −1, for instance, then the gender assortativity coefficient of this particular novel, and thus its amount of gender segregation, is relatively high.

Statistical baselines against which assortativity coefficients of individual novels can be compared are the average gender, age, education, and descent assortativity in the corpus. Table 1 shows that the mean gender assortativity is −0.11, which suggests that gender segregation in *De lichtekooi van Loven* (gender assortativity of −0.05) is in fact slightly on the higher end of the gender segregation spectrum. For each individual novel in the corpus, one could assess its relative degree of gender, age, education, and descent segregation by comparing it against the averages shown in this table.

Still, the question remains whether or not these averages themselves are relatively high or low. In order to answer that question, another baseline is required to compare these averages against. And although one could conduct a randomization test to create a baseline by performing N permutations on the data while keeping the ratios the same,[32] it seems strange not to frame this problem in terms of mimesis. While it is perfectly defensible to study fiction as textual objects in isolation from their societal context (as I primarily did in *Character Constellations*), this particular baseline problem calls for a

---

[32] For an extensive description of the set-up and results of the permutation test I conducted, see Smeets (2021). The outcome of the tests suggest that the average gender assortativity of −0.11 is just a random effect of the male–female ratio in the corpus and is not a sign of gender segregation or integration. For descent, education, and age this is the other way around. The relative positive descent assortativity of 0.18 is not a random effect of the ratio of characters with or without a migration background but suggests a relatively high amount of segregation by country of origin. The negative averages for the age and education assortativity coefficients are also not a random effect of the age and education distribution across characters in the corpus; rather, they signal a relatively high degree of integration rather than segregation for these variables.

Table 1 Descriptive statistics of the assortativity coefficients of gender, age, education, and descent in the Libris 2013 corpus (N=170).

	N	Minimum	Maximum	Mean	Std. Dev.
Gender assortativity	170	−1.00	1.00	−0.11	0.21
Age assortativity	170	−0.60	1.00	−0.07	0.26
Education assortativity	170	−0.50	1.00	−0.06	0.27
Descent assortativity	170	−0.61	1.00	0.18	0.48

Source: Smeets (2021).

comparison with social networks of people. Within the realm of social network analysis, techniques such as calculating assortativity to trace segregation are primarily applied to networks of people,[33] which makes it obvious to compare the results on segregation in these character networks with earlier studies on networks of people.[34] On a theoretical level, the debate on mimesis invokes the question to what extent these character networks are modeled on real-world examples. How likely is it that the degrees of segregation in a work of fiction reflect social divides in the society in which it was written?

Table 1 suggests that segregation by descent in the fictional worlds of the Libris 2013 corpus is relatively high (0.18) compared to segregation by gender (−0.11), age (−0.07), and education (−0.06).[35] An assessment of these results solely based on these numbers might lead to the conclusion that present-day Dutch literary fiction stages a considerable divide between characters with and without a migration background. As this seems to be in line with sociological studies on segregation by cultural background in networks of people (Marsden 1987; Marsden 1988), one might be inclined to consider this as evidence for a reflection theory: segregation by descent in society seems to seep through in the literary fiction written in that society. Given sociological findings on segregation, the results depicted in Table 1 thus do make sense. We cannot, however, simply assume that character networks have the same structure as networks of

---

[33] As far as I am aware, there is only one other study on fictional worlds using assortativity coefficients (Kraicer & Piper 2019).

[34] Sociological studies on segregation have targeted a range of variables, such as gender, cultural background, age, and education. Overall, there seems to be a consensus that segregation in general is high in networks of people, especially with regards to ethnicity and education, although differences have been observed (see Smeets 2021 for an extensive reflection).

[35] And this is also statistically backed up by the randomization test, the results of which are described in the previous footnote.

people. As we shall see, a systematic comparison between the character networks in this corpus and the networks of people in the same time period shows that literary fiction does not necessarily mirror social reality with regards to segregation patterns.

2.2.3 Libris 2013 versus SSND: Results (with Beate Volker)

Beate Volker and I have been working on such a systematic comparison in the period 2016–2019. As both of us had access to network data, on characters in present-day Dutch literature and on today's Dutch population respectively, the task of comparing these datasets at first glance seemed relatively straightforward – how similar are these character networks to the real-world networks? However, as I have argued, humans and characters are radically different as research objects. For that reason, one of the main challenges of our comparative study was to find a way to make our datasets comparable. This required a conceptual reflection on what fictional and real-world networks actually are, as well as a practical operationalization of how to compare them in a statistically sound way. Regarding the conceptual issue, we had to be mindful of the fact that social networks of people are commonly reconstructed in a very different way than character networks are. In Section 2.1, I discussed several approaches to character network extraction, of which the main issues are the definition of nodes (which entities to count as characters and which not?) and the definition of edges (e.g. based on conversation or on co-occurrences). While studies in the social sciences also vary in their approaches to delineating people's social networks, their definitions of nodes and edges tend to be more straightforward than is the case for character networks.

We compared the character networks within the Libris 2013 corpus to the Survey of the Social Networks of the Dutch (SSND), which is a survey-based longitudinal study of the social network in the Dutch population in the period 1999–2018.[36] These are the three main challenges we encountered in our comparison of the SSND dataset and the Libris 2013 dataset, as well as how we dealt with them:

1. The SSND is based on established survey methods to delineate personal networks from the respondents. So-called "name-generating questions" were used to ask respondents about the nature and the intensity of their contacts with people in their surroundings. For each of the respondents, the number of nodes in their personal networks depends on the people they

---

[36] For more information on the SSND, see Volker and Smeets (2019), section 3.1.1.

mentioned; the strength of the edges between the respondent and these mentioned people were determined by questions such as "with whom did you discuss important matters during the last six months?" (Marsden 1987). Obviously, such a survey-based approach to character network analysis is impossible as characters will not answer any of the questions you ask them. The delineation of character networks, conversely, does not depend on the information the research objects provide themselves, as is the case with networks of people, but instead relies on an external extraction of relations between characters based on their actual interactions at the level of the text. Unless one were able to delineate people's networks in a similar way, where one could trace people's interactions from birth to death, there is simply no way around this. As holds true for virtually every method or technique, both approaches contain a considerable amount of uncertainty that we have to live with. For instance, sociologists rely upon respondents' answers that are inevitably subjective and unstable (ask someone later and the answer will be different), whereas literary scholars are confined to what is (or is not) mentioned in a text as well as their deductions based on that information.

2. Survey-based network delineation methods such as those used for the SSND often have no other choice than to take the ego-centered networks of each of the respondents as a point of departure. In an ego network, only the relations of ego (i.e. the respondent) are established, but it is unknown if these relations themselves, referred to as "alters," are also connected. An example: if we ask Henk (ego) with whom he is connected, we get a list of alters with whom he is more or less strongly connected (Ingrid, Anita, Jan, Ali, Murat). As we did not ask these people with whom *they* are connected (because they did not take the survey), it is impossible to decide whether or not Ingrid and Anita, for instance, are also connected. For character networks based on co-occurrences, this *is* possible: connections between each of the detected characters are, for instance, established if they occur in the same two sentences. If Henk were a character in a novel, we would be able to determine the co-occurrence of his friends Ingrid and Anita, which might indicate whether or not they are also mutually connected. But this is not the case. In order to compare the SSND with the character networks in the Libris 2013 corpus, we therefore restructured the character networks in terms of ego-centered networks. Although we already knew whether or not any two characters in a novel were connected, we treated every character as a respondent taking a survey. For a novel with twenty detected characters, this resulted in twenty ego networks in which all relations to a particular character (ego) are delineated (see Figure 1).

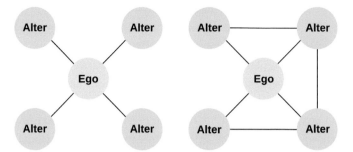

Figure 1 The ego-centered network on the left only features relations between ego and its alters, whereas the network on the right also features relations between alters. Adapted from Hansen et al. (2011).

3. The SSND network data was collected from a representative sample of the Dutch population at four points in time in the period 1999–2018. The character network data was collected from a representative sample of a "fictional population" of the characters populating books of Dutch literary fiction published in the year 2012 (all submitted to the Libris Prize 2013). Comparing networks of people with character networks not only requires the introduction of the concept of a fictional population; it also forces one to make explicit a theoretical assumption about mimesis and anti-mimesis. For the sake of convenience, let me state this in a binary way – although the matter is, in reality, gradual. If the reflection theory holds true, when exactly would one expect literary fiction to start reflecting social dynamics in the real world? In the case that segregation by country of descent is at a peak in Dutch society in the year 2010, for instance, how long approximately would it take until this network pattern leaves its traces in products of literary fiction written in that societal context? Conversely, if the social control theory holds true, when would one expect literary fiction to start influencing social dynamics? How long would it take until we saw the influence of books of literary fiction foregrounding narratives about ethnic or racial segregation (perhaps in the context of debates on migration and multiculturalism or by means of staging friendships and marriages between characters from differ-ent cultural backgrounds) on the dynamics between people from different countries of descent? Is it a matter of years or decades? While we are in the dark in terms of precise answers to these questions, for a first study it seems most convenient to compare networks of people with character networks in approximately the same time period. Taking into account that it takes some time for a book to be written and published, we decided to compare the character networks in the books published in 2012 with the third wave of

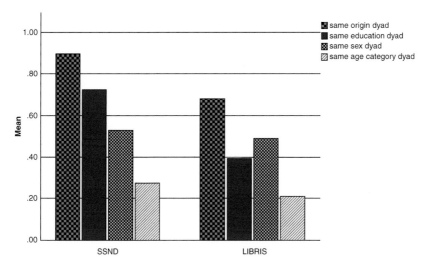

Figure 2 Similarity of dyads in networks of people and fictional characters (SSND n = 967 and LIBRIS n = 170).
Source: Volker and Smeets (2019).

data collection of the SSND from 2014, which comes closest to 2012. This phase of the data collection consisted of 1069 respondents.

Having dealt with these conceptual and practical issues, we thus compared the SSND and Libris 2013 by analyzing the extent of segregation by country of origin, level of education, gender, and age in both datasets.[37] In Figure 2, these divides are shown for each of the four variables in SSND and Libris 2013. The term "dyad" refers to connections between two people (SSND) or two characters (Libris 2013). If dyads of two people or two characters are similar with regards to country of origin, level of education, gender, or age, then the degree of segregation in their networks increases for these variables. For instance, if a respondent taking the survey (SSND) or a character in a novel (Libris 2013) is only connected to people with the same educational level, then segregation by education is 100 percent in their network because there is no interaction between people or characters with different educational levels. Figure 2 shows the mean values of these degrees in both datasets as a whole.

---

[37] This analysis was based on 65 percent (1297 characters) of the completed version of the Libris 2013 dataset (2137 characters). The data collection witnessed several phases, and this study was conducted in one of the earlier phases. For more information on the phases of data collection, see Smeets (2021). In this analysis, edges between characters were established based not on co-occurrences on the sentence level but on annotated metadata labels (such as friends, enemies, lovers, colleagues, family).

Breaking this down by each variable individually leads to some surprising insights in terms of mimesis. For each variable from right to left as they are presented in the graph, I will compare the scores in both datasets. First, segregation by age is the least present in both the SSND (about 27 percent) and Libris 2013 (about 20 percent). Social divides by age are thus slightly higher in the Dutch population than in Dutch literary fiction, with a small statistically significant difference.[38] Second, segregation by gender is almost the same in Dutch society and Dutch fiction, with degrees of about 50 percent in both the SSND and Libris 2013, the differences of which are not statistically significant. Third, segregation by education is considerably higher in the SSND (about 72 percent) than in Libris 2013 (about 40 percent), which is a highly statistically significant difference. Fourth, segregation by country of origin is also considerably higher in SSND (90 percent) than it is in Libris 2013 (68 percent), which is also a statistically significant difference. In sum, there is more segregation by age, education, and country of origin in personal networks within the Dutch population than there is in character networks in Dutch literary fiction. Character networks and networks of people are only alike with regards to segregation by gender.

How should we interpret these findings in terms of mimesis? In light of the reflection theory, the most straightforward interpretation is that Dutch literary fiction realistically reflects social dynamics with regards to gender segregation in Dutch society but does not reflect similar social dynamics with regards to segregation by age, education, and country of origin. But whereas there seems to be no literary imitation of these social divides, this indeed does not mean that for those types of social dynamics there is a situation of social control. The absence of a realistic reflection in fiction, in other words, obviously does not indicate a presence of control of fiction over society. While there can be various explanations of the fact that segregation by age, education, and country of origin is higher in Dutch society than it is in Dutch fiction, it is hard to make the case that the influence of fiction on society has something to do with that. Nonetheless, let me try to come up with an argument, which, theoretically speaking, could take at least two forms, one of which takes as its point of departure the past and the other the future.

From the perspective of the past, one could argue that the reason segregation by age, education, and country of origin is higher in Dutch society than in Dutch fiction is a result of earlier literary works that *did* stage fictional worlds with a relatively high degree of segregation with regards to these variables.

---

[38] For an extensive description of all statistical tests and significance scores, see Volker and Smeets (2019), section 4.2.

These earlier literary works then could have influenced segregation patterns in Dutch society to such an extent that this became part of social reality. Such an interpretation, however, is far-fetched for a few reasons. It assumes that literature has a dominant and determinative role in society that it arguably does not have. Only a small percentage of the Dutch population regularly read books,[39] and it also seems rather unlikely that people reading books would internalize these fictional social structures immediately and replicate them in their own social life – as if someone reading a book with many opposite-sex relations would automatically start to feel inclined to befriend someone of the opposite sex. This is not to say that literary fiction does not shape social reality in any way, just that it does not happen in such a direct and immediate way. Furthermore, it is unclear how long it would take for published books of literary fiction to have exercised some degree of influence on society. Besides, which society are we actually talking about? Literary fiction originally published in the Dutch language might also be read by people living in other countries and thus could also shape German, French, or Spanish social worlds.

From the perspective of the future, one could hypothesize that the relatively lower degree of segregation by age, education, and country of origin in Dutch literary fiction is like an omen, an indication of what to expect in the future. Although the Dutch population studied at the time (2014, the third wave of data collection in the SSND) was still stuck in the segregation patterns shown in the left part of Figure 2, their future social dynamics will follow the example set by the works of literary fiction published in the same time period. Literary fiction is a domain where the seemingly impossible or unimagined might take shape in various forms. With science fiction as an obvious example, authors of fiction are free to speculate about future worlds. Sometimes fiction is indeed ahead of the curve, like the novel *Little Women* (1868) by Louisa May Alcott, in which Josephine March becomes a successful professional writer, which makes her financially independent in an age where this was highly unusual for women. Many later female authors – including Simone de Beauvoir, Doris Lessing, Cynthia Ozick, Susan Sontag, J. K. Rowling, A. S. Byatt, and Margaret Atwood – claimed to have been inspired by the independence and perseverance displayed by Josephine March to become a writer (Acocella 2020).

However, the influence *Little Women* allegedly had on female authorship and women's emancipation is of a different kind than the influence segregation patterns in character networks may have on future social divides. This particular book with this particular character is famous for the blueprint it created for

---

[39] See https://digitaal.scp.nl/mediatijd/wie_leest_wat_en_hoe/ for a report on reading behavior in the Netherlands (last accessed July 14, 2021).

female authors of later generations who claimed to have been inspired by it. From their own accounts we might deduce that Atwood and Rowling internalized the ambitions of Josephine March and acted accordingly. Apart from such anecdotal evidence for one particular book and its alleged influence, there hardly seems to be an operationalizable method to trace how such a broad societal phenomenon as segregation is shaped or incited by its fictionalized manifestation in narrative form. In order to fill that gap, the final part of this section attempts to make sense of these character network analysis results by adopting a new formalist perspective.

2.2.4 Beyond the Reflection–Control Binary

What we do know is that there are considerable *differences* between segregation patterns in the Dutch population as opposed to the fictional population of characters in Dutch literature. For segregation by country of origin, the difference is particularly salient. At the very minimum, the comparative segregation scores shown in Figure 2 put the average assortativity coefficients shown in Table 1 into perspective. Without such a comparative perspective, one would have concluded that Dutch literary fiction is a domain in which identities with different cultural backgrounds do not really meet. That conclusion, however, is the result of judging literary fiction on its own standards, which, in light of a mimesis framework, is a one-dimensional text-centric approach that does not take into account *encounters* between aesthetic and social forms. At this point, the new formalism proposed by Caroline Levine (2015) seems particularly useful as a conceptual framework that might help to tie the knots. While it is clear that comparing segregation in aesthetic form with segregation in social form results in a different conclusion than only assessing segregation in aesthetic form (Figure 2 shows that character networks are considerably *less* segregated than social networks of people), it remains up for debate what the interaction between these two forms actually looks like.

Levine's new formalist framework allows for a nuanced interpretation of the interaction between fictional networks and networks of people. With her unusually wide definition of form – "all shapes and configurations, all ordering principles, all patterns of repetition and difference" (2015, 3) – and her uncommon conceptualization of interactions between forms, she opens up a refreshing way to reframe the relation between literary fiction and society. As my schematic sketch of the debate on mimesis from Plato to Oscar Wilde in the introductory section suggested, literary theory has not genuinely moved beyond the assumption that aesthetic and social form are separated, nor beyond the contention that one of these forms is dominant over the other. For Plato, the ground truth lies with "reality," whatever that may mean exactly, and literary reflections of that reality have not just a secondary but even a tertiary status (because it is only a reflection of a reflection of the universal forms in the realm of ideas). For Wilde, art and literature are primary because they exert influence over social and political forms. And while these positions only represent the extremes on the reflection–control spectrum (most literary scholars would be more nuanced about the matter), it seems safe to say that thinking in terms of this spectrum is common.

Levine traces such dialectical modes of thinking about the aesthetic and the social throughout the literary theory of the previous century. One of her main arguments is that "no form, however seemingly powerful, causes, dominates, or organizes all others" (2015, 16). Especially provocative is her criticism of Marxist perspectives on the interaction between forms:

> [Hayden] White contrasts reality – which he calls "social formations" – with the unreal coherence of narrative form. But if we understand social formations – such as the gender binary and the prison timetable – as themselves organizing forms, then we can see that White's real–unreal distinction does not hold. Literary forms and social formation are equally real in their capacity to organize materials, and equally *un*real in being artificial, contingent constraints. Instead of seeking to reveal the reality suppressed by literary forms, we can understand socio-political life as itself composed of a plurality of different forms, from narrative to marriage, from bureaucracy to racism. (Levine 2015, 14)

In this line of thinking, segregation is a form that interacts with various forms without being *caused* by any of these forms. With regards to the reflection–control binary, Levine would probably say that there is not an a priori dominance of social forms over aesthetic forms. There is rather a collision of different forms, and such collisions in turn create new forms. Her contention that none of these forms are less real than others is a serious threat to critical traditions, such as Marxism, that have assumed that one form lies at the root of other forms (e.g. social formations organizing narrative fiction).

Compared to Levine's new formalism, the literary scholarship on mimesis in the 1930s, 1940s, and 1950s (e.g. Inglis 1938; Berelson & Salter 1946; Barnett & Gruen 1948; Albrecht 1956) adheres to a more narrow conception of literary form. By using the reflection and social control theory as hypotheses to be either accepted or rejected, they conformed to a conceptual binary scheme in which either aesthetic form is caused by social form or vice versa. While also taking this binary scheme as a point of departure, my comparative analysis of the SSND and Libris 2013 indicates that it is particularly hard to convincingly argue for one of these forms as causing the other. This is not to say, however, that we cannot trace the ways in which forms *travel*, which, according to Levine, is one of the central features of forms. Instead of distinguishing between aesthetic form and social form in general, there is the possibility to more closely capture interactions between more detailed types of forms. What my comparative analysis makes clear is that segregation patterns are forms in themselves that collide with a range of other forms. In books of Dutch literary fiction, segregation patterns, in the first place, collide with narrative form and, more specifically, with the forms of narration, focalization, plot, and character. In the social experience of the Dutch population, the form of segregation collides with forms of social hierarchy present in Dutch society, such as the form of the gender binary. As forms in their own right, segregation patterns are thus manifested in both aesthetic and social form in a particular way without one being the root cause for the other.

Thinking about mimesis and the interaction between aesthetic and social forms along these lines replaces the notion of "causation" with that of "travel." Comparing segregation in characters networks with segregation in networks of people thus does not lead to any conclusions as to which are primary and which secondary but instead highlights the ways in which the form of segregation exists in the form of networks that are present in populations of both characters and people. Without assuming any form of causation, then, the broad question of how literary fiction and social reality interact still remains in place. "Fiction" and "reality," however, are less relevant categories, as "literary forms and social formation are equally real in their capacity to organize materials, and equally unreal in being artificial, contingent constraints" (Levine 2015, 14). But how, then, does the form of segregation in the literary and the social forms under scrutiny here "organize materials"?

Let me compare the form of segregation with the more apparent form of the gender binary to clarify how this might work in practice. Historically, the gender binary has organized many different forms – both aesthetic and social – in a variety of ways. One of its most visible aspects is the hierarchy it establishes between the male and the female. While, of course, not all gender binaries in literary history privilege the male over the female, the rich tradition of feminist literary criticism has shown that a particular expression of the gender binary – with the male as dominant – is present in a variety of cases (e.g. McEaston 2016). Something similar holds true for the manifestation of the gender binary in social forms. From at least the agricultural revolution onward, the female tends to be devalued in favor of the male in households, the workplace, politics, and so forth (Harari 2011, 161)[40] – while there are, indeed, many exceptions to that rule.

---

[40] "Different societies adopt different kinds of imagined hierarchies. Race is very important to modern Americans but was relatively insignificant to medieval Muslims. Caste was a matter of life and death in medieval India, whereas in modern Europe it is practically non-existent. One hierarchy, however, has been of supreme importance in all known human societies: the hierarchy of gender. People everywhere have divided themselves into men and women. And almost

Segregation patterns are perhaps more complex than gender binaries because it seems less obvious what their organizing qualities are – what they "afford," to speak with a term Levine uses. While it seems clear that gender binaries are powerful forms organizing both the aesthetic and the social in a particular hierarchical way, segregation patterns do not similarly speak for themselves. This is probably because segregation is inextricably entwined with the abstract form of the network: it is only in terms of network theory that we can understand the ways in which segregation structures relations between people or characters. Thus, we must first understand how networks work before we can understand how segregation works.

As I have repeatedly stressed in this section, character networks are of a different kind than networks of people. Not only does the ontological status of characters differ from that of human beings, comparative analysis of the SSND and Libris 2013 has demonstrated that network analysis of characters and people requires different methods and produces different results. While it seems safe to say that *characters* with a migration background are fictionalized expressions of *people* with a migration background, they are both embedded in the formal arrangement of the network in a very particular way. Unlike networks of people, character networks are inseparably linked to narrative form: we can trace interactions between characters on the sentence level, as the plot unfolds linearly and literary techniques of narration, focalization, irony, and metaphor are employed. The statistical differences between segregation in the SSND and Libris 2013 (Figure 2) might be explained by the ways in which narrative collides with networks and segregation. Focusing on such collisions at a micro-level reverts the logic of the reflection–control framework. While this binary logic is likely to result in unfruitful attempts to find a root cause for segregation (e.g. the absence of gender segregation in Libris 2013 is caused by a similar absence in the SSND), this alternative approach builds on the assumption that segregation is a form that preexists both aesthetic and social forms.[41] Segregation did not first exist in a population of people before it entered the realm of literary fiction; it is a form in its own right that is part of a dialogue with the forms of both character networks and networks of people. Not only can we learn something about segregation by studying how divides take shape in networks of people; we can also gain insight into segregation by tracing how it interacts

---

everywhere men have got the better deal, at least since the Agricultural Revolution" (Harari 2011, 161).

[41] According to Caroline Levine (2015), "narrative is an ideal form for avoiding metaphysical truth-claims about causes: it presents causality in something of the same way that it actually appears to us in the world, through an experience of unfolding" (135).

in literary fiction with narrative forms. How does segregation's collision with narrative forms (narration, focalization, plot, metaphor, irony) change the particular configuration of its own formal arrangement?

Answering that question will help to explain why, for instance, segregation by country of descent is high in both the Dutch population and Dutch literary fiction but considerably lower in the latter (see Figure 2). In order to understand it more fully, however, we have to move from the macro-level of the corpus to the micro-level of individual texts. It requires an in-depth analysis of the interaction of a wide variety of social and aesthetic forms that is simply impossible to conduct at the corpus level, because in every individual text these forms interact in their own unique way. While such a qualitative assessment of one novel is bound to be nongeneralizable for the corpus as a whole, it does help to gain insight into the complex interrelationships between segregation and other social and aesthetic forms. Without suggesting, then, that close reading provides a generalizable explanation of the differences in segregation between character networks and networks of people, it has the potential to demonstrate at the word, sentence, and text levels how collisions between a range of social and aesthetic forms in one particular narrative change the formal arrangement of segregation.

Furthermore, a more fine-grained analysis of a novel's discourse about, for instance, segregation and emancipation would generate more specific information about its relation to that particular societal theme. This is mostly due to the fact that qualitative readings of individual works enable one to take into account more narrative aspects at once than a quantitative network analysis can achieve. Indeed, a novel's relation to, for instance, segregation is represented not only by the structure of its character network but also by its characterization, thematic structure, symbolism, narration, and so on. Conversely, the affordance of the quantitative method proposed in the present section is that it enables one to gain insight into one particular narrative aspect (e.g. character network structure) in a way that covers more empirical ground than a qualitative analysis is ever able to do. By studying one quantifiable unit (the character network) of a representative sample of literary narratives (instead of a small selection of allegedly representative cases), I have been able to arrive at conclusions about segregation in literary fiction generalizable for a particular type of text in one particular period of Dutch literary history. In light of such conclusions (e.g. segregation by country of descent is high in both the Dutch population and Dutch literary fiction but considerably lower in the latter), I invite others to assess how particular novels conform to or deviate from that pattern by studying a wider range of narrative aspects in greater detail.

3 Novel Connectivity: Female Characters and Women's Emancipation

Whereas the previous section discussed the imitative dimension of character networks synchronically, focusing on one year of literary production, the current section aims to trace a historical shift in literary representation by comparing character networks from two distinct periods of Dutch literary history: the 1960s and the 2010s. In order to gain insight into the ways in which character networks transform as social reality changes across a period of approximately fifty years, I will compare two corpora of Dutch-language novels in light of one particular sociohistorical development: women's emancipation. Without suggesting that the emancipation of women necessarily evolves linearly, I hypothesize that the network centrality of female fictional characters increases as two consecutive feminist waves enter the sociopolitical landscape.[42] Building on the findings from the previous section, this section takes as a vantage point the idea that formal arrangements such as the gender binary are prone to change while both aesthetic and social forms collide. Before testing this hypothesis through a comparative character network analysis, I will provide a brief scholarly background on the history of women's emancipation and the changing role of "the female" in (Dutch) literary history. Taking this theoretical framework as its point of departure, Section 3.2 then analyzes the network position of female characters in the 1960s and the 2010s in light of the historical developments outlined in Section 3.1.

3.1 Women's Emancipation, Female Writers, Female Characters

Although a wide variety of earlier examples are known of women who have been standing up for their rights from at least the Middle Ages onward (Meijer 1994, 90), the history of women's emancipation tends to be divided into three distinct historical moments. While each nation has a unique history in this regard,[43] the first feminist wave is considered to have taken place in the late nineteenth century. For the Dutch situation, Aletta Jacobs and Wilhelmina Drucker are particularly famous for having paved the way for women's right to vote and their access to higher education and paid employment. While elsewhere the second wave gained momentum considerably earlier, in the

---

[42] While it is common to distinguish several waves of feminist activity, the "waves" metaphor has received criticism, amongst other reasons because it suggests that women's emancipation has evolved linearly in distinct periods (Laughlin et al. 2010).

[43] In 2017, market research company Ipsos published a report on feminism and gender equality in twenty-four countries: www.ipsos.com/en-hk/feminism-and-gender-equality-around-world (last accessed June 16, 2021).

1960s,[44] in the Netherlands the movement witnessed its peak in the 1970s and early 1980s. Both Joke Smit's manifesto "Het onbehagen bij de vrouw" (1967) and Anja Meulenbelt's book *De schaamte voorbij* (1976) are often considered as having sparked Dutch second-wave feminism. While the first wave primarily targeted equal rights to education and paid employment, second-wave feminists also addressed a wider range of topics, including divorce and reproductive rights.

Although critiques by third-wave feminists from the 1990s to the 2010s of the ideas of second-wave feminists in the 1960s, 1970s, and 1980s show that feminism has adopted many forms and emphasized a variety of different issues over the years,[45] it seems safe to say that the social awareness around women's rights has drastically changed between the 1960s and the 2010s. The yearly published "emancipation monitor" by Statistics Netherlands (Centraal Bureau voor de Statistiek), furthermore, shows that the societal position of women has steadily improved in terms of employment, pay equity, and distribution of childcare, even if continuing disparities still leave room for improvement.[46] Although it is hard to pinpoint exactly how feminist thought has affected women's emancipation on these specific issues,[47] it seems clear that it has contributed to the awareness of gender issues and related policies.

---

[44] Heavily influenced by Simone de Beauvoir's *La Deuxième Sexe* (1948), Betty Friedan's *The Feminine Mystique* (1963) is often regarded as having kick-started second-wave feminism in the United States.

[45] From the 1990s onward, third-wave feminism emerged as a critical response to the second wave. As "a new discourse or paradigm for framing and understanding gender relations that grew out of a critique of the inadequacies of the second wave" (Archer Mann & Huffman 2005, 60), third-wave feminism should be understood as "against" rather than "after" the second wave. Whereas the second wave was a continuation and broadening of the debates on women's rights triggered by first-wave feminists, the third wave distinguishes itself from the previous wave along at least four lines. First, scholars such as Patricia Hill Collins addressed the ways in which the intersection of different categories of identity (e.g. gender, class, race, sexuality) work together to cause other forms of inequality previously unaddressed by second-wave feminism. Second, postmodernist and poststructuralist critics went one step further and "used difference to deconstruct all group categories and to reject oppositional thinking" (Archer Mann & Huffman 2005, 62). Third, feminist postcolonial and global feminist critics such as Gayatri Spivak (1990) highlighted "the potency of historical specificity" and wanted to simultaneously "rescue collective categories and avoid essentialism" (Archer Mann & Huffman 2005, 67). Fourth, younger-generation feminists drew on earlier feminist waves to address a wide variety of new topics, perspectives, and angles while agreeing that their feminist predecessors were "too judgmental and restrictive" (69).

[46] See www.cbs.nl/nl-nl/dossier/dossier-emancipatie (last accessed June 22, 2021). This linear narrative of women's emancipation (in the Netherlands) has been criticized from a "post-feminist" perspective: see www.radboudrecharge.nl/nl/artikel/gelijke-kansen-voor-iedereen-nou-nee-dus (last accessed June 22, 2021).

[47] In her doctoral thesis, Elizabeth Shannon (1997) has provided an extensive account of how feminist thought has contributed to policy changes in Ireland and Australia with regards to abortion and equal pay.

Literary scholarship has not failed to acknowledge the interrelations between feminist movements and the position of "the female" in literary history. Perhaps most famously, Elaine Showalter has provided extensive accounts of the changing roles of women writers from the 1800s onward. Focusing on the history of British novelists, her seminal study *A Literature of Their Own* (1977) starts from the assumption that "it is important to see the female literary tradition in these broad terms, in relation to the wider evolution of women's self-awareness and to the ways in which any minority group finds its direction of self-expression relative to a dominant society, because we cannot show a pattern of deliberate progress and accumulation" (11). Building on three different historical phases of female authorship she distinguished in this book, Showalter extends her inquiry in *A Jury of Her Peers* (2009) to American women writers while adding a fourth phase:

> First, there is a "a prolonged phase of imitation of the prevailing modes of the dominant tradition"; second, "there is a phase of protest" against these modes, and "advocacy" of independent rights and values; and third, a phase of self-discovery, a search for identity and a specific aesthetic. I called these phases in women's writing "feminine," "feminist," and "female." In the 1970s, I could only imagine a fourth stage, a "seamless participation in the literary mainstream." By the end of the twentieth century, however, American women's literature had reached the fourth and final stage, which I would now call "free." American women writers in the twenty-first century can take on any subject they want, in any form they choose. (xvii)

Although Showalter does not connect these four phases in literary history explicitly to the waves of the feminist movement, there are parallels between these aesthetic and sociopolitical developments in terms of their historical situatedness. The first phase of feminine literature is characterized by women born between 1800 and 1820 who were allegedly still imitating "the prevailing modes of the dominant [male] tradition." This makes sense if one takes into account the fact that their works – published in the decades around the mid-nineteenth century – obviously could not have been influenced by first-wave feminism, as that movement only started to take root around the end of the nineteenth century. The next feminist phase (women born between 1820 and 1840 whose books allegedly conveyed "protest" and "advocacy") and female phase (women born between 1840 and 1860 whose books expressed "self-discovery" and a "search for identity") have arguably evolved in relative conjunction with the emergence of the first wave of women's emancipation. Finally, the free phase takes shape in the same period that witnessed the rise of third-wave feminism.

Whereas Showalter does not make any direct claims with regards to the specific dynamic between the aesthetic forms of women's writing and the social forms of the feminist movement, other literary scholars have more explicitly written about the ways in which one of these forms might be the root cause for the other. For Dutch literary history,[48] Maaike Meijer acknowledges both elements of reflection and social control within Dutch literary texts published around the peak of second wave feminism in the Netherlands:

> Since the 1970s, literary texts have played an invaluable role in constructing women's identity. The feminist movement had – and still has – an effect on literature worldwide. I see feminist literary bestsellers not only as a *reflection* of feminist thought. The labels "reflection" or "imitation" are connoted too passively. They suggest that literary production is the terminal station of feminism, but that does not do justice to the effect this literature has on reality, nor to the politicizing effect it has on its readership. One might also say that the feminist movement not only took shape in personal lives, not only in social, political, and economic domains, but also in literature. (Meijer 1994, 99; emphases in original text)[49]

In her inaugural lecture (1995), Maaike Meijer expands on the dynamic between the feminist movement and representations of feminist ideas in high literary culture as well as in popular culture. Particularly salient is her claim that second-wave feminism has been "prepared" in both higher and lower forms of cultural productions in the Netherlands: "The 1950s and 1960s witnessed the emergence of a *textual climate*, a conglomerate of texts and images in which emerging social changes were prepared, registered, edited, and answered" (Meijer 1995, 5).[50] Central to her reasoning is her observation that popular cultural expressions, such as songs on the radio, played a more vital role in the early representation of feminist ideas than high forms of literary fiction. Unlike female song-writers, "literary women's writings had to compete with an often sexist literary criticism and a male dominated literary establishment" (19),[51] which in turn hampered the distribution of feminist ideas in high literary culture. And perhaps as a result of these gender biases in Dutch literary institutions, "[Dutch] mainstream writers are considerably misogynistic," while "feminist visions were more likely to be found in the writings of Hella Haasse and

---

[48] While I consider Maaike Meijer an iconic scholar of Dutch literature and author gender, there has been a wide range of other high-quality studies on the topic, with some of the most important being Boven (1992), Vos (2008), Bel and Vaessens (2010), and Koolen (2018).

[49] All translations from Dutch to English are my own.

[50] "Er ontstond in de jaren vijftig en vooral zestig een *tekstklimaat,* een heel conglomeraat van teksten en beelden waarin beginnende sociale veranderingen werden voorbereid, geregistreerd, verwerkt en beantwoord."

[51] "Ze hebben daarbij een verspreiding, een populariteit en een invloed die veel groter was dan die de literaire schrijfsters in de jaren vijftig en zestig konden bereiken. De schrijfsters moesten in die decennia altijd opboksen tegen een niet zelden seksistische literaire kritiek en een mannelijk gedomineerd literair establishment."

Andreas Burnier, as well as in the writings of female authors who achieved a less canonical status, such as Nel Noordzij, Ankie Peypers, and Aya Zikken" (7).[52]

In light of the mimesis debate, it is significant that Meijer uses the term "pretext" to denote "the concrete text that can be indicated as a concrete precursor, as a powerful model for the new text" (30).[53] For the Dutch situation, this new text is the manifesto *Het onbehagen bij de vrouw* [The woman's discomfort] (1967), in which feminist Joke Smit famously put the issues of second-wave feminism on the Dutch political agenda. Although this manifesto is usually considered to have triggered the feminist movement in the Netherlands, there have been a range of pretexts within popular song culture that already in the earlier years of the 1960s addressed the issues Smit raised (Meijer 1995, 16). Meijer thus acknowledges the influence that the aesthetic forms of the pretexts had on social forms that increasingly changed as a result of the awareness of gender inequality – social forms that would soon be incorporated within changing policies regarding, for instance, reproductive rights.[54]

While Meijer's theoretical reflections on the dynamic between the feminist movement and feminist cultural production is a source of inspiration for the comparative character network analysis presented in Section 3.2, her claims raise questions with regards to mimesis and the reflection–control binary. More specifically, her conclusions about pretexts that prepared or shaped later feminist ideas in the public debate invoke two interrelated questions with regards to the comparative character network analysis I will present. First, to what extent are the novels from the early years of the 1960s pretexts for ideas of the second-wave feminism that gained momentum in the 1970s? Second, to what extent do these higher forms of literary fiction differ from the lower forms of popular songs Meijer addresses? In terms of their publication date, it is perfectly possible that the novels published in the early 1960s are pretexts of new feminist texts such as Joke Smit's famous manifesto. In light of Meijer's claims, however, it remains to be seen whether or not writers that are part of the male-dominated literary establishment are likely to voice feminist ideas.

A more specific question concerns the relation between the societal position of women and the network centrality of female characters. While literary scholars such as Showalter and Meijer acknowledge a relation between women's writing and the social awareness around gender inequality, there are,

---

[52] "De mannelijke mainstream schrijvers zijn behoorlijk misogyn. Feministische visies zijn eerder aan te treffen bij auteurs als Hella Haasse en Andreas Burnier, en bij vrouwelijke auteurs die een minder gecanoniseerde status bereikten, als Nel Noordzij, Ankie Peijpers en Aya Zikken."

[53] "[Daarom] stel ik voor 'pretekst' te reserveren voor de concrete tekst die aangewezen kan worden als concrete voorloper, als machtig model voor de nieuwe tekst."

[54] In 1984, abortion was legalized in the Netherlands by means of the "Wet afbreking zwangerschap" (Law for aborting pregnancy).

to the best of my knowledge, no data-driven studies into the ways female characters in fiction have changed as the societal position of women was improving.[55] There are, however, a few qualitative studies thematizing this relation. Focusing on a selection of feminist fiction writers, such as Margaret Atwood and Doris Lessing, Gayle Green provides an account of the genre of feminist fiction between the 1960s and 1980s as an important broker of feminist thought. Based on qualitative assessment of some representative examples, Neal Curtis and Valentina Cardo (2017) suggest that representations of female characters in superhero comics "mark an intervention on behalf of female creators in keeping with the theory and practice of third-wave feminism" (381). In *Middlebrow Feminism in Classic British Detective Fiction* (2013), Melissa Schaub argues that the "frequently occurring character, which [Schaub calls] the Female Gentleman, is a representative example of the unrecognized feminism of middlebrow British novels" (1), which she interprets as a response to the social changes instigated by the feminist movement. For theatre in the 1880s up until the 1920s, Susan A. Glenn makes the case in *Female Spectacle: The Theatrical Roots of Modern Feminisn* (2002) that the women's characters played by female performers were crucial for the spread of feminist ideas and the emergence of second-wave feminism.

Although scholars such as Greene, Curtis and Cardo, Schaub, and Glenn make connections between the aesthetic form of the female character and the social forms of women's emancipation, their research focuses on female (feminist) writers specifically and not on (literary) fiction more broadly. And while there are a modest number of data-driven studies on the status of female characters in film (e.g Agarwal et al. 2015; Pennel & Behm-Morowitz 2015) and video games (e.g. Lynch et al. 2016) more broadly, these do not address gender representations systematically in terms of mimesis and women's emancipation.[56] In Section 3.2 I aim to fill this research gap by conducting a comparative character network analysis on collections of books published in the 1960s and the 2010s against the background of the emergence of second- and third-wave feminism.

3.2 Network Centrality of Female Characters: 1960s versus 2010s

Does the position of female characters transform during the period of approximately fifty years in which the position of women in society changed due to

---

[55] The study by Underwood et al. (2018) is perhaps one of the few exceptions, although they do not explicitly theorize this relation. In Section 3.2 I will discuss the importance of this study for the present research.

[56] More recently, Michelle Moravec and Kent K. Chang (2021) published an article that fits within a mimesis framework. In it, they examine the extent of influence six American feminist bestsellers might have had on contemporary discourse.

emancipatory movements of second- and third-wave feminism? If it does, what does this particular dynamic between aesthetic and social forms tell us about mimesis? In this section, I will approach these questions by testing the hypothesis that the centrality of female characters in Dutch literary fiction increases between the 1960s and the 2010s as the societal position of women improves. This hypothesis is premised on the argument that the network centrality of fictional characters has a particular relation to the emancipation of the social group they represent. Without suggesting that this is a one-on-one relation (network centrality and emancipation are obviously not the same) or that other narrative aspects are less relevant, network centrality can be considered as a quantitative proxy for the prestige, authority, or importance characters have in the fictional society of which they are part.

Although they do focus not on network centrality but on characterization, a similar hypothesis is tested by Ted Underwood, David Bamman, and Sabrina Lee (2018) for a corpus of 104,000 works of English-language fiction between 1703 and 2009. The comparative character network analysis presented in this section takes some of their findings as its point of departure. While Underwood, Bamman, and Lee do not explicitly theorize their findings in light of the ebb and flow of the three feminist waves, they hypothesize that "the prominence of female characters ... would have increased in the nineteenth and twentieth centuries – with, to be sure, some well-known interruptions" (4). Their expectation to "see an overall story of progress across two centuries" (ibid.) is reasonable if one assumes that aesthetic forms (literary narratives, characterization) evolve in relative conjunction with social forms (the status of women in all kinds of societal domains). But their research shows that the dynamic relation between the aesthetic and the social has been evolving less linearly than expected. For the period of 1800 to 1960, the percentage of words used to describe female characters in English-language fiction declined steadily. This runs counter to a reflection theory of mimesis: the improved societal status of women as a result of first-wave feminism is apparently not reflected in the visibility of female characters in terms of characterization.

On a smaller scale (two corpora of, respectively, 155 books from the 1960s and 170 books from the 2010s) and for a different language area (Dutch-language fiction), I also test the hypothesis that aesthetic and social forms linearly evolve in a parallel fashion. Whereas Underwood and his coauthors operationalize the significance of gender in fiction in terms of characterization, I focus on network centrality. Although it is unclear how characterization and network centrality exactly relate to one another, it seems safe to say that they are two different ways of measuring the "importance" of characters – the first particularly in discursive terms, the second more specifically in terms of network theory.[57] In network theory, centrality is operationalized by a range of network centrality metrics, each of which stresses a different network-related aspect.[58]

For the period that I will be comparing, the 1960s through the 2010s, a particularly significant finding of Underwood et al. is that the decline of words used to describe female characters reverses around 1970, for reasons that might have to do with the emergence of second-wave feminism, although the authors do not explicitly make that connection. If this reversal also holds true for network centrality, we might expect to find that the network centrality of female characters increases between the 1960s and the 2010s.

Another finding of this study that is relevant for my present inquiry is the effect that author gender appears to have on the textual representation of gender. As authors tend to write about characters who have the same gender as their creators, the decline of published female authors from the middle of the nineteenth century to the middle of the twentieth century seems to have caused a decline in the number of female characters as well (Underwood et al. 2018, 5). For present-day Dutch-language fiction, I earlier demonstrated with Lucas van der Deijl, Saskia Pieterse, and Marion Prinse that there is a similar relation between author gender and character gender in the Libris 2013 corpus: men

---

[57] It should be mentioned that there are various other quantitative techniques within the realm of Digital Literary Studies that could be used to assess the hypothesis that "the female" becomes increasingly important in the last two centuries of literary history. Apart from my network analysis approach and the discursive approach by Underwood et al. (2018), one could consider, for instance, topic modeling (how do topics associated with "the female" change over time?), sentiment analysis (how do more positively or negatively connoted descriptions of female characters change over time?), or machine-learning-based text classification (how stable is the division between "female" and "male" descriptions?).

[58] Network theory has produced a wide range of centrality metrics that can be used to statistically assess the importance of a node in a network. Degree centrality is the most straightforward of those metrics: it defines the importance of nodes in terms of the amount of relations it has with other nodes – a node with a lot of edges has a high degree of centrality, whereas a node with only a few edges has a low degree of centrality. Sociologist Linton Freeman (1978) has been famous for introducing betweenness centrality and closeness centrality as additional metrics. Unlike degree centrality, the metrics of betweenness and closeness define centrality in terms of a node's position in the network instead of the number of edges it has. Nodes with high betweenness centrality are often called "brokers": they are central because they connect different parts of the network that would not be connected if one removes the broker. This is often demonstrated by the fact that communication between the two distinct parts of the network fully depends on the existence of a node with high betweenness. While closeness centrality similarly depends on network position, it is not defined in terms of brokerage but in terms of distance. A node with high closeness is central because it is closest to all other nodes in the network. Next to degree, betweenness, and closeness, metrics based on vector centrality are among the most widely used (e.g. Katz centrality and Google's PageRank centrality are variations on eigenvector centrality). This metric is based on a circular assumption: nodes are considered more influential if they are connected to other nodes with high eigenvector centrality. Unlike eigenvector centrality, Katz centrality tends to be more useful for networks that are not strongly connected.

write more often about men, and women more often about women – although the pattern for female authors is less strong than for male authors (van der Deijl et al. 2016). Because of these two findings, I will test not only the effect period of publication (1960s versus 2010s) has on the network centrality of characters but also what the effects of author gender are. It could very well be that the year in which a novel has been published has less to do with the centrality of its female characters than with the gender of its author. For the mimesis debate, it is worthwhile to assess these different levels at which imitation between aesthetic and social forms take place.

Before delving into the results of the comparative network analysis, I first discuss the preprocessing steps that were necessary to produce high-quality corpora and related datasets of semiautomatically identified characters.

3.2.1 Corpora, Data, Methods (with Jurrian Kooiman and Nils Lommerde)

In order to compare the centrality of female characters in Dutch-language novels in the 1960s with those from the 2010s, it was necessary to obtain two representative corpora from these periods. For the 2010s, we used the same Libris 2013 corpus (170 novels published in 2012) that I used in earlier studies and for which extensive demographic metadata (gender, country of descent, age, education, profession) on each of the 2137 identified characters is stored in an open-access database.[59] As stated earlier, these 170 novels represent 37 percent of all originally published Dutch-language books in the category of literary fiction. In an ideal world, we would have created a second corpus of a similar, highly representative amount of Dutch literary fiction from one particular year in the 1960s, preferably all submissions to the Libris Prize 1963 or a related prize for Dutch literary fiction. Unfortunately, this ideal world does not exist. The Libris Prize was only established in 1993 and awarded from 1994 onward. There were, furthermore, predominantly oeuvre prizes for Dutch literature in the 1960s, with no prizes similar to the Libris system of bulk lists, longlists and shortlists.

Another challenge is the digital availability of Dutch literary fiction from the 1960s. Most of the books published in the period are not freely accessible online due to copyright regulations; some authors are still alive, while others are dead but not yet for for seventy years or more (not long enough for their works to enter public domain, in other words). Furthermore, the largest share of these books has not been digitized at all. Whereas most novels published in the last decade or so are similarly published on paper and in the digital-born format of the ePub, publishing houses are not systematically producing e-books of works

---

[59] See section 2 ("Corpus and dataset") for more information on the Libris 2013 corpus and dataset.

they published more than half a century ago – and if they are, it is most of the time only for books having already achieved a highly canonical status.

To tackle these practical problems, we had to be pragmatic while simultaneously meeting methodological standards. In order to produce a corpus of 1960s Dutch literature that can be compared to the Libris 2013 corpus, we had to make sure that we were not comparing apples to oranges. Our corpus selection and preprocessing strategy consisted of four consecutive phases:

1) Because of the sparse availability of e-books from the 1960s and the lack of a substantive, freely accessible digitized collection from that period,[60] we first intended to produce digital versions of a selection of books by manually digitizing them. While making plans for carrying out such an extremely time-consuming project, we were informed that historian of language Ewoud Sanders had been working on an extensive private collection of digitized Dutch-language materials. We were very fortunate to have been given access to this collection, which dismissed the necessity to scan books ourselves.

2) The Ewoud Sanders collection of digitized materials consists of a highly diverse variety of Dutch-language sources from the Middle Ages up until the present, including works of literary fiction, historical fiction, poetry, and nonfiction. From this broad collection, we singled out a corpus comparable to the Libris 2013 corpus in terms of publication year, genre, and size. First, we isolated all sources published in 1962, precisely fifty years earlier than the 2012 novels in the Libris 2013 corpus. Second, we isolated the books of literary fiction for adults by removing all materials that could not be categorized as such.[61] Third, as the books published in 1962 conforming to these criteria were not as many as we hoped, we also included the years 1961, 1963, 1964, and 1965. This resulted in a corpus of 155 books of literary fiction originally published in the Dutch language in the period 1961 to 1965, which I hereafter will call the ES (Ewoud Sanders) 1960s corpus. After consulting with the Royal Library of the Netherlands (Koninklijke Bibliotheek), we estimated that this corpus makes up a representative portion of all originally published literary fiction in the Dutch-language area from this time period, which is comparable to the Libris 2013 corpus.[62]

---

[60] The Digital Library for Dutch Literature (Digitale Bibliotheek voor de Nederlandse Letteren) only contains a handful of novels from the 1960s.

[61] In the Dutch-language area, the system of NUR-codes to categorize books in distinct genres was only created in 2002, which meant that we could not simply look for NUR-code 301 (literary fiction).

[62] Whereas the Libris 2013 corpus represents 37 percent of Dutch-language literary fiction originally published in one year, the ES 1960s corpus represents 27 percent of Dutch-language literary fiction originally published in five years in the early 1960s (1961, 1962, 1963, 1964, 1965). It is

3) As the Ewoud Sanders collection has been created on pragmatic grounds, we introduced one further criterion (apart from genre, publication year, and corpus size). As the Libris 2013 corpus consists of books that are considered by their publishers as high-quality fiction that could possibly gain official recognition by winning the Libris Prize, the ES 1960s corpus should at least contain the most recognized books in the period 1961 to 1965. As such, we made an inventory of the most acknowledged, highbrow, canonical authors based on prize-winning authors who published in the early 1960s as well as those who are mentioned in the most recent Dutch literary history, *Altijd weer vogels die nesten beginnen. Geschiedenis van de Nederlandse literatuur 1945–2005*, by Hugo Brems (2006).[63] This helped to confirm that the books by the majority of the highbrow authors publishing between 1961 and 1965 were already present in the ES 1960s corpus. Only six books that conformed to this criterion were not. For those books, we purchased the available ePub versions.

4) For the Libris 2013 corpus there were no issues with the quality of the texts because there existed born-digital versions. Most books in that corpus were simultaneously published on paper and as an e-book, and for those books of which only a paper edition was published I acquired a digital version (in plain text, Word or PDF format) by contacting the publisher or the author directly. This was different for the books in the ES 1960s corpus as the majority of the digitized versions were acquired by manually scanning from paper. In order to have machine-readable versions of these scans, Optical Character Recognition (OCR) was used,[64] which inevitably results in less than 100 percent accuracy. Some of these errors are structural and predictable (e.g. the letter "m" is often mistaken for "rn"), while others are rare and unpredictable (e.g. seemingly random spaces between the letters of a word). Although it should be noted that the OCR quality of the ES 1960s corpus was already relatively high at first instance,[65] post-OCR corrections could

---

important to note that, like Western literary production more broadly, Dutch literary production grew immensely between the 1960s and the 2010s. This is also clear from the percentages mentioned here. While the samples are comparable in absolute numbers (155 versus 170 books), the Libris 2013 corpus covers a larger percentage of a shorter period than the ES 1960s corpus (one versus five years of literary production).

[63] Freely accessible via www.dbnl.org/titels/titel.php?id=brem012alti01 (last accessed May 7, 2021).

[64] Optical Character Recognition is a widely used technique to make the text of digitized books searchable and analyzable. Adding a layer of OCR to digitized books is a necessary requirement for any form of computational text analysis.

[65] It was qualitatively estimated at between 90 percent and 95 percent, which is in line with systematic evaluations of OCR quality (Govindan & Shivaprasad 1990), with some notable exceptions.

enhance the quality. While the best quality is commonly achieved by manually correcting errors, we chose to perform automatic post-OCR corrections to spare time and effort. We were fortunate to have been assisted by a group of students enrolled in Radboud University's Data Science Project course,[66] who used a combination of machine learning techniques and a dictionary look-up approach to develop a custom-made post-OCR pipeline for this corpus specifically. This enhanced the quality drastically.[67] Furthermore, while most books in the ES 1960s corpus did not have a digital-born version at the time they were scanned, a considerable amount appeared to have been published as e-books later on. To have the best quality available, we purchased those e-books as well. In total, 30 of the 155 books in the corpus were accessible as e-books (and thus represent perfect text quality), while the OCR quality of the remaining 125 books was automatically corrected using the software devised by these students.

In order to conduct the comparative network analysis, character networks were semiautomatically extracted from both the ES 1960s corpus and the Libris 2013 corpus using the approach developed earlier (Smeets 2021).[68] For the Libris 2013 corpus, we worked with the ready-to-use dataset of demographic metadata – gender, country of origin, education, age, profession – on the 2137 identified characters in the 170 novels.[69] For the ES 1960s corpus, we created a similar dataset from scratch.

As this approach relies on demographic metadata that cannot be detected automatically, computer-oriented analysis was combined with evaluation by two expert-annotators in these two ways:

1. Character detection

   For each of the 152 novels in the ES 1960s corpus, a list of named entities was automatically produced using the NER functionality from Python's spaCy library.[70] After this list was narrowed down to only those named

---

[66] Many thanks to Tamara Mauro, Floris Cos, Annemijn van Klink, Boudewijn Schiermeier, and Iskaj Janssen, who worked on this project between February 2021 and June 2021.

[67] See this GitHub repository for more info on this post-OCR approach, their qualitative evaluation, and a link to their software: https://github.com/FlorisCos/DSP_OCR_improvement_algorithm (last accessed July 13, 2021). Based on a qualitative evaluation of their approach for three novels (with born-digital e-books as a baseline), they report improvements in the Character Error rates (CER) ranging from 6.1 percent to 64.7 percent and improvements in the Word Error rates (WER) ranging from 3.4 percent to 35 percent.

[68] See Section 2.1 ("Character Network Analysis: Premises, Methods, Techniques") for an extensive reflection on this approach.

[69] See https://github.com/roelsmeets/character-networks for all code and data.

[70] spaCy is a freely available, widely used software package that can be used for different natural-language processing purposes: see https://spacy.io/ (last accessed May 11, 2021). For all code used in this paragraph, see https://github.com/roelsmeets/actual-fictions.

entities falling into the "Person" category, two expert annotators manually corrected the list by means of a cursory examination of each individual novel. Those characters without a name or whose name was not automatically detected by the NER software were added to the list, while those named entities not referring to a character were removed. Taking into account Zipf's law,[71] only those characters who are part of the N most frequently occurring characters were incorporated in the final list. This resulted in a list of 2164 identified characters,[72] a number which is close to the 2137 identified characters in the Libris 2013 corpus. Using the first list of automatically detected named entities as their point of departure, these expert annotators also collected name variants of each individual character (e.g. "Frits," "Frits van Egters," "Van Egters," "Fritsje," "Frizzle"),[73] which were subsequently used to automatically detect the positions in the texts where these characters occur.

2. Gender resolution

   While the dataset of the Libris 2013 contains a wide range of demographic metadata (gender, country of origin, education, age, profession), only information on character gender is required for the present comparison between Libris 2013 and ES 1960s. Based on lists of popular Dutch male and female names from the Corpus of First Names in the Netherlands (*Nederlandse Voornamenbank*),[74] it was automatically estimated whether a character falls into one of three gender categories (male, female, gender neutral). These automatically generated results were subsequently evaluated by the two expert annotators who confirmed whether or not these estimations were right and manually corrected the errors. This resulted in gender metadata for each of the 2164 identified characters in the ES 1960s corpus.[75]

3.2.2 Results of Comparative Network Analysis: 1960s versus 2010s

Do female characters in Dutch literature become more or less central over time when comparing the 1960s to the 2010s? How can we interpret the answer to that question in light of the rise and peak of Dutch second- and third-wave feminism? In order to answer these questions, I will discuss the results of a range of statistical tests.

---

[71] See Section 2 ("Character Network Analysis: Premises, Methods, Techniques"), for a reflection on taking into account only the N most frequently occurring characters.

[72] See NODES_AF.csv in https://github.com/roelsmeets/actual-fictions.

[73] See NAMES_AF.csv in https://github.com/roelsmeets/actual-fictions.

[74] See www.meertens.knaw.nl/nvb/english/ (last accessed May 11, 2021).

[75] See NODES_AF.csv in https://github.com/roelsmeets/actual-fictions.

I hypothesize that the centrality of female characters compared to male characters increases between the 1960s and the 2010s. This hypothesis is based on a simple and possibly naïve reflection theory stating that a stronger presence of women in Dutch society translates to more central female characters in Dutch literary fiction. While Underwood et al. (2018) demonstrated for English-language fiction that, contrary to their expectations, the importance of female characters in terms of characterization has not evolved linearly (see the introduction to paragraph 3.2 in that work), my earlier analysis of network centrality in the Libris 2013 corpus does provide a reason to expect that female characters in the 1960s are less central than those in the 2010s. One of my earlier findings demonstrated that the female characters in the Libris 2013 corpus are more central than their male counterparts, at least on two of five centrality metrics that I tested (Smeets, Sanders & van den Bosch 2019; Smeets 2021). This ran counter to my expectations in two ways. First, the close-reading-based tradition of critiques of Dutch literary representation has provided extensive accounts of the gender biases and stereotypical representations in Dutch literature at the expense of the female. I expected that this would translate to a lesser importance, dominance, or influence of female characters in statistical terms, which appeared not to be the case. Second, female characters in the Libris 2013 corpus are significantly less visible as they occur significantly less often than male characters (40 percent female, 60 percent male). Similarly, this lack of visibility led me to expect that female characters would be less central in terms of network theory as well, which also turned out to be incorrect.

Let me start with some descriptive statistics. Although I am particularly interested in the *network centrality* of female characters, frequency of occurrence is a first indication of the importance of the female in both corpora. Figure 3 demonstrates that the male–female ratio of characters between the 1960s and the 2010s is surprisingly stable – perhaps even "depressingly stable" (10), to borrow a phrasing from Underwood et al. (2018). Interestingly, distributions of character gender around of 60:40 and 70:30 (male-to-female) have been observed in a variety of corpora across language fields and time periods (e.g. van der Deijl et al. 2016; Kraicer & Piper 2019). Such ratios (close to 2:1) have been referred to by Eve Kraicer and Andrew Piper as "the golden mean of patriarchy" (2019, 3), which suggests a law of literary representation that seems not to have been affected by social transformations such as women's emancipation.[76] For the present case study, the simple descriptive statistic that women are staged almost as often in the 1960s as in the 2010s raises serious

---

[76] In popular fiction (Hollywood films, Netflix series, and so on), comparable gender ratios are found, with some extreme exceptions, such as the complete absence of female characters in *The Hobbit*: https://the-digital-reader.com/2015/09/14/infographic-gender-ratio-in-popular-fiction/ (last accessed June 8, 2021).

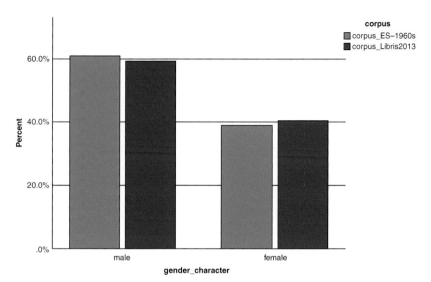

Figure 3 Distributions of character gender in Sanders 1960s (N=2164) and Libris 2013 (N=2137)

doubts for a reflection theory of mimesis. Notwithstanding the increasingly strong positions of women in Dutch society, they are still significantly under-represented in highbrow Dutch-language fiction. In terms of visibility of the female, little has changed in a period of Dutch literary history co-occurring with second- and third-wave feminism.

Running a range of statistical tests to determine if the network centrality of female characters compared to male characters changes between the 1960s and the 2010s does not radically alter that picture. A statistical test apt for this goal is the two-way ANOVA, which can be used to assess whether or not there is an interaction between two independent variables on a dependent variable.[77] In order to examine the effect of character gender (male or female) and corpus (Sanders 1960s or Libris 2013) on network centrality, two-way ANOVAs were conducted for five network centrality metrics: degree, betweenness, closeness, eigenvector, and katz.[78] No statistically significant interactions between the effects of character gender and corpus on network centrality were found for the first four of these metrics. This means that, between the 1960s and the 2010s, female characters compared to male characters do not have increasing *numbers of interactions* with other characters (degree); are not increasingly *brokers* connecting remote parts of the network (betweenness); are not increasingly *embedded* in their networks

---

[77] For a more extensive explanation of this statistical technique, see https://statistics.laerd.com/ spss-tutorials/two-way-anova-using-spss-statistics.php (last accessed January 10, 2022).

[78] See footnote 58 for an explanation of these five centrality metrics.

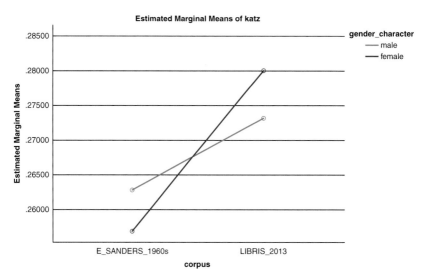

Figure 4 Two-way ANOVA with Katz centrality as dependent variable and character gender and corpus as independent variables

(closeness); and are not increasingly connected to *other more central* characters (eigenvector).

A statistically significant interaction was only found for Katz centrality, F (1, 4291) = 15.541, $p < 0.001$, which is illustrated in Figure 4 by the crossing of the two lines of character gender and corpus. While eigenvector and Katz centrality are based on similarly circular logic stating that the centrality of a node increases if it is "upvoted" by other nodes with high centrality (which is how Google partly ranks its web pages by using the similar PageRank centrality), Katz increases for female characters in this period of approximately fifty years while eigenvector does not. One explanation for this difference is that Katz tends to work better for networks that are not fully connected, which is the case for most networks of fictional characters (the mean density in Libris 2013, for instance, is 0.50, which is modest but far from high). Taking into account the small effect size (i.e. the proportion of variance in the data explained by this interaction effect) made me decide to disregard this finding as a confirmation of our hypothesis that the network centrality of female characters increases between the 1960s and the 2010s. While a η^2 of 0.01 already indicates a small effect size,[79] the η^2 of 0.004 for this two-way ANOVA is much smaller than that. Furthermore, the

---

[79] In statistics, $\eta2 = 0.01$ is considered a small effect size, $\eta2 = 0.06$ a medium effect size, and $\eta2 = 0.14$ a large effect size.

fact that four out of five two-way ANOVA tests do not produce statistically significant interaction effects between character gender and corpus is an even stronger argument to not confirm but reject the hypothesis.

While the network centrality of female characters thus does not seem to increase between the 1960s and the 2010s, a rather salient finding is that the network centrality of *all* characters increases between these two time periods, irrespective of gender. Statistically significant main effects of corpus were found for all five metrics.[80] Figure 5 illustrates that there is an upward trend for each of the five centrality metrics. Overall, over a period of approximately fifty years, characters in Dutch-language fiction come to have *more* interactions with other characters (degree); have higher chances to be *brokers* (betweenness); be more *embedded* in their networks (closeness); and have more interactions with *other central* characters (eigenvector and Katz). This has little to do with gender, which is visually illustrated by the fact that the two lines in each graph representing male versus female characters do not obviously cross. As demonstrated, Katz centrality is the only exception to this rule, with a statistically significant interaction effect between character gender and corpus, although with an extremely small effect size. And whereas the lines of male and female characters slightly cross in the graphs for degree and betweenness, their interaction effects are not statistically significant.

Whereas the gender of characters has no effect on the increasing network centralities of characters, we have not yet rejected or confirmed the theory that the gender of *authors* has had an effect on these upward trends, as there are several studies showing that author gender is an important variable in such matters (van der Deijl et al. 2016; Underwood et al. 2018; Koolen 2018). As there is no reason to expect that author gender interacts differently with character gender in the 1960s than in the 2010s, we run a two-way ANOVA for both corpora separately. In order to examine the effect of character gender (male or female) and author gender (male or female) on network centrality, two-way ANOVAs were thus conducted for the five network centrality metrics (degree, betweenness, closeness, eigenvector, and katz).

For the 1960s corpus, no statistically significant interaction effects between character gender and author gender were found. This means that male and female authors in the 1960s do *not* ascribe more central network positions to

---

[80] Main effect of corpus for degree centrality: $F(1,4291) = 135.819, p < 0.0001$, partial $\eta2 = 0.031$. Main effect of corpus for betweenness centrality: $F(1,4291) = 59.926, p < 0.0001$, partial $\eta2 = 0.014$. Main effect of corpus for closeness centrality: $F(1,4291) = 4.741, p = 0.029$, partial $\eta2 = 0.001$. Main effect of corpus for eigenvector centrality: $F(1,4291) = 2.863, p = 0.091$, partial $\eta2 = 0.001$. Main effect of corpus for katz centrality: $F(1,4291) = 103.433, p < 0.0001$, partial $\eta2 = 0.024$.

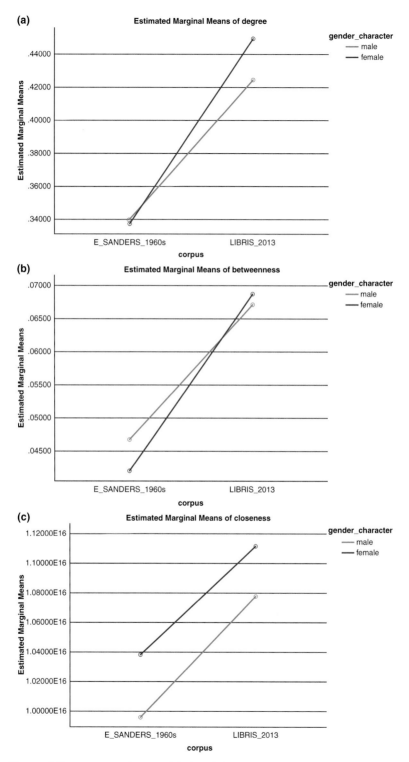

Figure 5 Two-way ANOVAs with the all five centrality metrics as dependent variables and character gender and corpus as independent variables

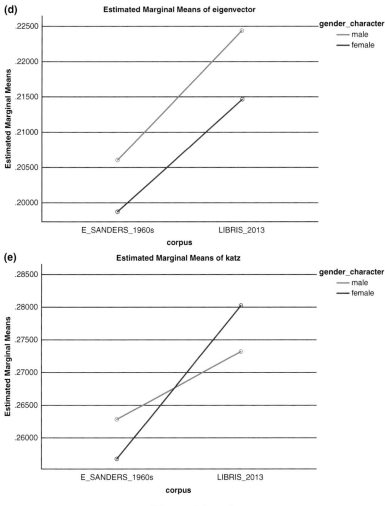

Figure 5 (cont.)

either male or female characters. The gender of the author in this period has, in other words, nothing to do with how central male and female characters are in narrative fiction.

This is slightly different for the 2010s corpus. Whereas there is no statistically significant interaction effect between character gender and author gender for degree, betweenness, and katz centrality, there is an interaction effect between these variables for closeness and eigenvector centrality. In the 2010s, author gender, therefore, does not affect the *number* of interactions male and female characters have (degree); does not affect the extent to which male and female characters are *brokers* (betweenness); and does not affect the extent to

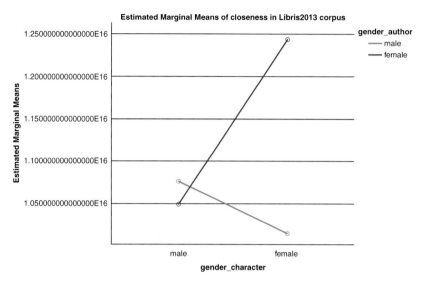

Figure 6 Two-way ANOVA conducted on the Libris 2013 corpus with closeness centrality as dependent variable and character gender and author gender as independent variables

which male and female characters are connected to *other more central* characters (Katz). In this period, however, the gender of authors does have an effect on how *embedded* male and female characters are in their networks (closeness), $F(1, 2073) = 5.280$, $p = 0.022$, partial $\eta2 = 0.003$. In more recent Dutch literature, male characters have higher scores on closeness centrality in books written by male authors, whereas female characters score higher on this metric in books by female authors (see Figure 6).[81]

Something similar holds for eigenvector centrality (see Figure 7). In the 2010s, the gender of authors seems to have an effect on the extent to which male and female characters are connected to *other more central* characters in terms of eigenvector centrality, $F (1, 2073) = 4.544$, $p = 0.033$, partial $\eta2 = 0.002$. As with closeness centrality, authors in this period tend to implicitly ascribe more central positions to characters who share their gender. In books written by male authors, male characters on average score 0.231 on eigenvector centrality whereas female characters score 0.207. In books written by female authors, conversely, female characters on average score 0.232 on eigenvector centrality and male characters only 0.203.

---

[81] On average, male characters in *books by male authors* score 1.076E+16 on closeness and female characters only 1.049E+16. Conversely, female characters in *books by female authors* score 1.243E+16 on this metric and male characters only 1.016E+16.

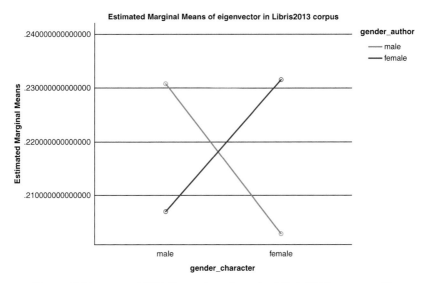

Figure 7 Two-way ANOVA conducted on the Libris2013 corpus with eigenvector centrality as dependent variable and character gender and author gender as independent variables

In sum, these findings partially reject and partially confirm the hypothesis that author gender has an effect on the network centrality of female and male characters. The evidence to the contrary, however, is most convincing. For Dutch fiction in the 1960s, the network centrality of male and female characters does not depend at all on whether the book was written by a male or a female author. In the 2010s, this also holds true for three out of five centrality metrics (degree, betweenness, katz). For two out of five metrics (closeness, eigenvector), there is a statistically significant interaction effect between author gender and character gender. In this period, more specifically, male authors tend to ascribe more central positions to male characters and female authors more central positions to female characters on these two metrics. This is in line with findings from other studies suggesting that authors write differently about characters who share their gender (e.g. van der Deijl et al. 2016; Underwood et al. 2018). Taking into account the extremely small effect sizes of the two tests (out of five) that reached statistical significance, however, we have to be careful to draw general conclusions. The respective $\eta2$'s of 0.003 (closeness) and 0.002 (eigenvector) are below the threshold of 0.01 (indicating a small effect size) and thus should be considered extremely small – only a very small share of the variance in the data is thus explained by these two interaction effects between author gender and character gender. As such, it seems safe to say that the gender of authors has only a very small part to play in the network centrality of male and female characters in Dutch fiction from both the 1960s and the 2010s.

Taken together, the results of the statistical tests reported here challenge earlier theories about the influence literary texts might have had on women's emancipation. We should reconsider, for instance, Maaike Meijer's claim that second-wave feminism has been "prepared" in popular songs and literary texts (1995, 5). If feminist thought indeed took root in textual culture, no traces of those "roots" are found in the position of female characters in their social networks. While it might be true that literary texts from the early 1960s were "pretexts" of the feminist movement on other levels, fictionalized women in books of Dutch literary fiction were no role models for the feminist movement in the sense that they were both significantly less visible than their male counterparts (40:60 ratio) and had no major roles in their social networks. In terms of mimesis, this raises doubts about Meijer's social control theory that textual culture sparked second-wave feminism and laid the foundation for a new phase of women's emancipation (1994, 99). This might, however, have something to do with both the publication date and the genre of these books. Perhaps books published in the early 1960s might have simply been too early to have put a mark on the feminist movement in the Netherlands, which only really took off in the 1970s. Furthermore, Meijer (1995, 19) has claimed that, unlike popular songs, highbrow literature (such as the books in the Sanders 1960s corpus) were part of a male-dominated literature culture, which might have resulted in more conservative gender dynamics or a slower emancipation in terms of female characters.

Conversely, these findings also challenge a reflection theory of mimesis. Although it is tempting to produce a linear narrative in which the position of fictionalized women increasingly improves as women of flesh and blood are increasingly emancipated, the present study provides no evidence for that. This is in line with Underwood et al. (2018), whose findings on characterization also contradict a similar linear narrative about women's emancipation and its effect on fiction. But while a story of linear progress with regards to gender seems unlikely, Figure 5 does suggest that there is an upward trend in terms of social networking in general. In the final part of this section, I will provide an explanation of this pattern in terms of mimesis and, more specifically, in light of Levine's new formalist framework.

3.2.3 Radical Relationism

Needless to say, Dutch society witnessed enormous social, political, cultural, and economic transformations between the 1960s and the 2010s. In a period of fifty years, the world changed drastically. As a response to the new possibilities of Dutch postwar society opened up by economic prosperity and the lifting of religious and sociopolitical barriers, a youth culture emerged in the early 1960s, of which Jan Cremer's bestseller *Ik Jan Cremer* (1964; also in the Sanders 1960s corpus) became a symbol. According to historian Hans Righart, the problems both the postwar and the prewar generation faced while adapting to this new world resulted in a "double generation crisis" (1995). Furthermore, as described in more detail in Section 3.1, second-wave feminism in the 1970s and the early 1980s raised awareness of gender inequality and strengthened the position of women on the socioeconomic hierarchy, while third-wave feminism from the 1990s onward further addressed and problematized issues of identity in the widest sense.

Without discrediting the importance of these and other developments (e.g. economic growth and crisis, the Cold War and its cessation, revolutions in the arts), perhaps the most radical change had to do with connectivity. In all kinds of ways, the world between the 1960s and the 2010s became more connected: faster and cheaper means of transportation; the advent and popularization of communication technologies (telephones, the internet, smartphones) and new media (television, social media); and the globalization of economic trade all combined to shape a world where people were granted seemingly endless possibilities for travel, communication, and business. Seen in that light, one might conclude that Dutch literary fiction becomes more relational, more connected, more networked by referring to a reflection theory of mimesis. The simple rationale would be this: the increasing importance of the unit of the social network in fiction (see Figure 5) is a reflection of the broader evolution of social networks in the (Western) world at large.

This explanation fits perfectly with a literary-historical development that has been described with a variety of terms by scholars trying to make sense of literary culture after postmodernism. While scholars have been approaching that question from different angles and have emphasized different aspects of the "new" literature, scholars seem to agree by now that contemporary literature has slowly but surely been moving away from the postmodernist practices of solipsism and irony toward a renewed sense of community building and sincerity in relations to others. With the label "cosmodernism," for instance, literary scholar Christian Moraru puts emphasis on the "concept and practices of 'relationality'" (2011, 3) of more present forms of literature. In a similar vein, the term "new sincerity," often associated with the likes of David Foster Wallace, Zadie Smith, Dave Eggers, and Jonathan Franzen (Kelly 2010), foregrounds this move away from postmodernist irony and toward authentic relations with self and others. Literary scholars Hans Demeyer and Sven Vitse (2020) have characterized the generation of millennial authors publishing in the 2010s with the term "affective crisis": instead of epistemological questions (modernism) and ontological questions (postmodernism), the newer generation poses affective questions and emphasizes feelings, relationality, and attachment.

Specifically for Dutch-language fiction, Yra van Dijk and Merlijn Olnon (2015) have coined the term "radical relationism" to describe the "search for new forms of relational identity" in novels written by Dutch authors from the millennial generation.[82] These "relational novels" contain a few basic characteristics:

> These novels are not only about protagonists who do or do not engage with the world, who do or do not know themselves, who do or do not form durable relations, but mainly about the realization that relations with others are a precondition for our identity. . . .
> For the young characters in these novels, in other words, it is not about developing authentic, personal, uniform identities, but instead about cultivating the realization that identities are necessarily constructed, relational, and pluriform.[83]

Unlike modernist novels exploring the limits and possibilities of individual consciousness and postmodernist novels questioning the very nature of being, contemporary novels move beyond such radical forms of philosophical skepticism and instead focus on how to be part of a social network, a community, a collective. Narratives of literary-historical developments like this one (from modernism to postmodernism to post-postmodernism, cosmodernism, or radical relationism) are appealing not only because they are coherent and overarching but also because they can be understood in light of other social, cultural, and economic trends. The attraction to such coherent narratives, in other words, seems heavily indebted to a reflection theory of mimesis that assumes that literary fiction transforms as the contexts it is produced and functions in change. For present-day fiction, the reflection theory states that the "relational novel" and its foregrounding of "networked identity" grew out of a response to increasing relationality and connectivity in the world at large. And while, of course, there might be some form of social control at play here as well, it seems unlikely that relational novels had a crucial impact on, for instance, globalization.

---

[82] "'Radicaal relationisme' duidt dan niet zozeer op nieuwe of meer relaties tussen personages als wel op het zoeken naar nieuwe vormen van een relationele identiteit."

[83] "Het gaat hier niet alleen om hoofdpersonen die zich wel of niet engageren, zichzelf wel of niet kennen, zich wel of niet binden, maar vooral om het besef dat voor onze identiteit het in relatie zijn met anderen een voorwaarde is. . . . Oftewel, het gaat bij de jonge personages in deze romans niet om het ontwikkelen van authentieke, persoonlijke, eenduidige identiteiten, maar juist om het cultiveren van het besef dat identiteiten per definitie geconstrueerd, relationeel en meerduidig zijn."

Thus, our finding that Dutch fiction becomes more networked can be explained by labels such as "cosmodernism" (Moraru), "affective crisis" (Demeyer and Vitse), or "radical relationism" (Van Dijk and Olnon) that refer to other social, cultural, or economic contexts to which these artistic trends might have been a response in one way or another. Being mindful of Caroline Levine's new formalist framework (see Section 2.1), I should, however, apply a few crucial nuances, especially in light of the rejection of the hypothesis that female characters became more central between then and now. While it is tempting to explain the overall increase of network centrality of characters between the 1960s and the 2010s as a reflection of the growing importance of networks in the world at large, to do so would be to adopt a binary theory of social and aesthetic forms – to assume that the social and the aesthetic can be separated into two distinct domains that might reflect or influence one another. In practice, however, it seems more likely that they overlap and interact more organically. Levine would say, furthermore, that the formal arrangement of the network binary preexists its expression in both the aesthetic form of literary fiction and the social form of interaction between people of flesh and blood. The increase of networked identity in both Dutch fiction and society is thus not a matter of one being the root cause of the other.

This is, of course, not to say that one form cannot dominate or organize another one. As I have already pointed out in Section 2.2.4, the formal arrangement of the gender binary seems to be a dominant, organizing form in both the social and the aesthetic domain. More particularly, the female has been structurally devalued in favor of the male in the course of social, political, economic, and cultural history (Harari 2011, 161). Similarly, literary history has witnessed a seemingly constant hierarchical organization of the gender binary: from the social dynamic between Adam and Eve onward, the male has been portrayed as morally superior to the female in literary fiction.[84] Obviously, this is not a rule without exceptions. But while there is, of course, a wide variety of books that challenge the gender hierarchy,[85] structural gender biases seem to be part of the very DNA of narrative fiction, which is, amongst other things, expressed through the lesser presence, the marginalization, and the stereotypical portrayal of female characters.

---

[84] See https://mceaston.com/2016/01/23/the-western-literary-canon-or-the-curious-case-of-the-male-ego/ (last accessed June 22, 2021).

[85] Two obvious examples, some of which I have also mentioned in the previous section: *Little Women* (1868) by Louisa May Alcott features Josephine March, who challenges nineteenth century gender norms; and Margaret Atwood is famous for her critical reflections on hierarchical organizations of gender, for instance in *The Handmaid's Tale* (1985).

Indeed, a gender bias is not unique to narrative fiction or the arts more broadly. As a form, the gender binary has also been pervasive in its hierarchical organization of the female and the male in the sociopolitical domain. However, the history of women's emancipation has demonstrated that this hierarchy can change, although sometimes extremely slowly. While women are still disadvantaged in a variety of aspects, their legal rights and societal status today are incomparable to the situation 200 years ago. The findings of this section, however, suggest that the manifestation of the gender binary in Dutch literary fiction is more stable in the aesthetic than in the sociopolitical domain. The fact that the gender of characters does not interact in a statistically significant way with the overall increase in network centrality between the 1960s and the 2010s indicates that the gender binary has not genuinely changed on the level of literary representation. In terms of network theory, there is no upsurge of "strong" female characters in the period following two feminist waves. Women, in other words, seem to have been less emancipated in literary fiction than in real life.

This finding is incompatible with the last, "free phase" of women's writing that contemporary fiction finds itself in according to Elain Showalter (see Section 3.1). Although she is discussing American women's writing specifically and not literary fiction in general, her claim that "American women writers in the twenty-first century can take on any subject they want, in any form they choose" (2009, xvii) is disputable in light of the empirical evidence presented in this section. If, for the sake of argument, we assume that Dutch literary fiction is not radically different from American literary fiction, this section's findings contest the idea that twenty-first-century literary fiction is "free" in the sense of not being restricted by biased gender norms. This works on two levels. First, the form of the gender binary has been relatively stable across a period of fifty years. Not only is "the golden mean of patriarchy" (Kraicer & Piper 2019, 3) visible in the almost unchanged ratios of male versus female characters in this period, gender has also no effect on the increasing network centrality of characters between the 1960s and the 2010s (see Figure 5). Second, the gender of authors has only a small, and perhaps negligible, part in the increase of network centrality (see Figures 6 and 7). Although two out of ten statistical tests produced a significant interaction effect between author gender and character gender, female characters in both the 1960s and the 2010s seem, generally speaking, no more central in the works of female authors than they are in the works of male authors. Although gender norms in the literary field are, obviously, also manifested in other variables than network centrality or frequency of occurrence of female characters, the stability of the gender binary with regards to these two variables (period of publication, author gender) challenge

Showalter's linear narrative about women's emancipation in literary history. Has twenty-first-century literary fiction really arrived in a "free phase" if the social dynamics between male and female characters have been affected so little by second- and third-wave feminism?

4 Conclusion

4.1 Actual Fictions

When the French critic Marc Fumaroli characterized Michel Houellebecq as a "baromètre sociale" in *Le Point* (Fumaroli 2005), he referred to the writer's seemingly magical power to capture a sociopolitical climate in prose *before* its excesses were manifested in day-to-day reality. Published just before 9/11, his novel *Plateforme* (2001) concludes with religious extremists attacking a sex resort in Thailand, a plot twist that would be compared to the Bali bombings a year later. More recently, his Islam-critical novel *Soumission* (2015) made international headlines because of the grim coincidence that it was published on the day of the *Charlie Hebdo* shootings. Notwithstanding the fierce criticism Houellebecq has received for the reactionary elements of his works,[86] the odd convergence of his literary narratives with social reality gained him the reputation of a writer ahead of his time whose works not just follow but determine what happens in the world.

Although there exists a variety of other authors who, like Houellebecq, seem to have "predicted" historical events,[87] it is fairly easy to discredit such examples as a rare twist of fate. Nonetheless, the idea that fiction is a valuable source for better understanding social reality is far from an absurd idea. Recently, literary scholar Jurgen Wertheimer was asked by the German Ministry of Defence to help predict the next war by examining large collections of literary works.[88] Despite government funding for his Project Cassandra being terminated at an early stage, the demand for such a project shows that mimesis is also a topic of interest outside faculties of arts. Not only can we understand fiction better by studying its relations to society; we can also learn something about society by studying its relations to fiction. And although predicting wars by researching literature sounds highly ambitious and perhaps even grotesque,

---

[86] E.g. Martin Gelin, 'The Prophet of the Far Right', *The Boston Review*, May 15, 2020 (http://bostonreview.net/arts-society/martin-gelin-prophet-far-right, last accessed July 8, 2021).

[87] To name two of the most famous: H. G. Wells's *The World Set Free* (1914) contains references to what was later compared to atomic bombs; and George Orwell famously wrote in *1984* (1949) about a surveillance culture not far removed from certain present-day state surveillance programs.

[88] In an interview in *The Guardian*, Wertheimer emphasizes "literature's ability to identify a social mood and cast it into the future" (Oltermann 2021).

the core assumption behind Project Cassandra – that fiction and reality influence one another – runs like a red thread through the history of literary theory.

The idea that literary narratives may contain signals of something that has happened or is about to happen has been the vantage point of this Element. Unlike Project Cassandra, however, the goal was not to signal dramatic historical events such as wars but to pinpoint how social dynamics within Dutch society are manifested in the interactions between both fictional characters and people of flesh and blood. By systematically comparing character networks to social networks of people, this Element has contributed to a closer understanding of how the aesthetic and the social converge or diverge. In doing so, *Actual Fictions* attempts to move beyond the mysticism associated with terms such as "baromètre sociale" used for Houellebecq (Fumaroli 2005) and instead provide data-driven insights into the specific ways in which *forms* such as the network organize fiction and reality. Moreover, it demonstrates how computational techniques and statistical analysis are valuable tools for rethinking an age-old concept such as mimesis. Moving away from famous examples of literary fiction writers who unmistakably put their mark on social reality (e.g. Michel Houellebecq, Harriet Beecher Stowe, J. J. Cremer), the present study empirically tested two hypotheses about mimesis on two corpora of Dutch fiction in the 1960s and the 2010s.

Actual Fictions makes two central claims. First, studying literary fiction against the background of larger political and sociological trends reveals similarities and differences between the aesthetic and the social. By systematically comparing character networks to networks of the Dutch population in a given period (the 2010s), Section 2 demonstrated how social divides along the lines of gender, country of origin, education, and age are organized differently in the aesthetic and the social domains. While my previous work studied segregation in character networks on their own terms (Smeets 2021), focusing on the literary texts in relative isolation from societal trends, the present study – based on joint work with sociologist Beate Volker – puts these findings in perspective. Whereas my earlier study suggested that levels of segregation by cultural background, and to a lesser extent by education and age, are high in Dutch fiction, the present study arrived at a different conclusion. Segregation by cultural background is high in fiction but significantly lower than it is in the Dutch population. This is not to say that these earlier results on segregation in character networks are invalid or meaningless, but rather that they should be interpreted differently when compared to social networks of people. Taking on such a fundamental mimetic approach leads, in this case, to a more nuanced interpretation about networks. Indeed, segregation by cultural background is high in both fiction and society, but it is less so in literary fiction, which suggests that literary narratives set an example of what a more connected, less divided world could look like.

Second, we should be skeptical about linear literary-historical narratives suggesting that the aesthetic evolves in a parallel fashion with the social (e.g. Showalter 2009). Unlike my synchronic approach in the section on segregation in the 2010s, the section on feminism presented a historically comparative approach to character networks. Focusing on second- and third-wave feminism, Section 3 tested the hypothesis that the network centrality of female characters increases between the 1960s and the 2010s. This hypothesis makes sense from the perspective of a reflection theory of mimesis stating that literary fiction mirrors or follows societal trends. In a period of fifty years in which the societal position of women increasingly improves, we might expect female characters to play more central roles in narrative fiction as well. Earlier, Underwood et al. (2018) demonstrated that this assumption does not necessarily hold true when tested for large corpora of English-language fiction. Where this earlier study found that, over time, female characters do not gain more narrative space in terms of characterization, my findings on network centrality equally contradict such a reflection theory. A salient finding of this section is that the network centrality of *all* characters increases between the 1960s and the 2010s, which I have interpreted as an indication of the emergence of the post-postmodern "relational novel" (Van Dijk & Olnon 2015). However, this effect seems to be independent of character gender. Challenging such a linear literary-historical narrative about women's emancipation (in fiction), this section emphasizes that there may be some forms, such as the gender binary, that appear relatively stable across time periods. More concretely, the network position of female characters does not evolve along with the emancipation of women in society. Furthermore, female characters remain peripheral in terms of visibility, with gender ratios close to 2:1 (male to female) being observed across language areas and times periods (e.g. Underwood et al. 2018; Kraicer & Piper 2019; Smeets 2021). This is an important finding. It suggests that books of literary fiction contain conservative elements and that narratives do not necessarily change along with broader societal developments such as women's emancipation.

Taken together, the findings from these two sections challenge ingrained, primarily theoretical ideas about how mimesis more broadly, and literary realism more specifically, works. In the first place, the data-driven approach developed in this Element helps to pinpoint the differences and similarities between the social and the aesthetic by adhering to the values of representativity and generalizability. Unlike most theoretical accounts of mimesis from Plato onward, *Actual Fictions* relied on the strategy of hypothesis testing, opening up the possibility to not only confirm but also *reject* presumptions about mimesis and literary realism. It is easy to see how Plato, for instance, might have arrived at a reflection theory of mimesis given the fact that it fits perfectly in his metaphysical system. But whereas the armchair philosophy method was probably sufficient for his goals, the field of cultural analytics excels at avoiding potential confirmation biases by seeking computational-statistical models that most convincingly "fit" empirical observations.

And indeed, some findings of the Element contradict intuitions one might have about dynamics between the aesthetic and the social. This is also true with regards to some of my own intuitions, assumptions, and expectations. Most unexpected is my finding that second- and third-wave feminism seems to have had little effect on the importance of the female in Dutch fiction. Ideological approaches to literature have repeatedly shown how hierarchies of gender, race, class, and so on organize narrative fiction even up to this day, but I was struck by the extent to which such qualitative findings were confirmed on a large scale in the present study. All the available evidence suggests that the hierarchical organization of the gender binary is surprisingly stable in the aesthetic domain – that literary fiction seems to have moved along so little with social reality in that respect. My surprise was probably due to one of these widespread, canonical ideas about mimesis found across the history of literary theory, from Plato to Wilde to Fumaroli. While such ideas have greatly influenced Western thought about fiction's relation to the world with grand phrases such as "art mirrors life" (Plato), "life imitates art" (Wilde), and "baromètre sociale" (Fumaroli), they are very rarely contested by means of empirical hypothesis testing. Of course, not all grand theories of art have to be weighted on a statistical scale – sometimes we need theory for theory's sake. Furthermore, when the empirical evidence runs counter to these theories, they are not necessarily useless or invalid. Plato's, Wilde's, and Fumaroli's ideas constitute a range of theoretical positions within discussions of mimesis that can be used as points of departure for further inquiry.

Actual Fictions, however, demonstrates that, when such theories are tested empirically, the results may change our understanding of a concept we thought we understood. Mimesis is such a fundamental and all-encompassing concept in literary theory that we might take it for granted. For most literary scholars, it probably goes without saying that there is a certain dynamic between literary fiction and social reality, whether it is in the form of reflection or control or, more often, something in between those two extremes. We see a societal trend or concern and we assume fiction responds to it in one way or another. The 2010s, for example, witnessed a rise in climate fiction novels thematizing the dramatic effects of climate change on life on planet Earth. While this seems a perfect example of a reflection theory of mimesis, it is far from a foregone conclusion as to what this dynamic between fiction and social reality actually looks like. So-called "Cli-Fi" novels echo a topic of major societal concern, but it is not clear from the start how these should be positioned on the reflection–control spectrum or, to speak with Caroline Levine, which forms organize others in both the aesthetic and the social domains. In order to understand how such dynamics work, we should, in other words, try to make explicit how *actual* these fictions are.

Also, for those theoretical strands that elicit a particular theory of mimesis (e.g. Marxist approaches presuming a reflection theory), it tends to be unclear which assumptions about mimesis are at play and, if so, how they can be put to the test. Conversely, *Actual Fictions* proposes to get it all out on the table, to make explicit what often remains implicit. Following Caroline Levine (2015), its approach has been an attempt to move beyond the either/or logic of historicist versus formalist perspectives on art and culture. Character network analysis is just one of the ways in which computational techniques and statistical analysis can help to pinpoint how forms interact, converge, diverge, or clash.

References

Abrams, Meyer Howard. *The Mirror and the Lamp: Romantic Theory and the Critical Tradition.* Oxford: Oxford University Press, 1953.

Acocella, Joan. "What's lost and gained in a modern 'Little Women'." *New Yorker*, February 7, 2020. www.newyorker.com/culture/cultural-com ment/whats-lost-and-gained-in-a-modern-little-women.

Agarwal, A., J. Zheng, S. Kamath, S. Balasubramanian, and S. A. Dey. "Key female characters in film have more to talk about besides men: Automating the Bechdel Test." In *Proceedings of the 2015 Conference of the North American Chapter of the Association for Computational Linguistics: Human Language Technologies*, pp. 830–840. Denver, CO: Association for Computational Linguistics, 2015.

Alberich, R., J. Miro-Julia, and F. Rossello. "Marvel Universe looks almost like a real social network." Elsevier Preprint, 2002. Retrieved from http://arxiv .org/abs/cond-mat/0202174.

Albrecht, Milton. "Does literature reflect common values?" *American Sociological Review* 21, no. 6 (1956): 722–729.

Auerbach, Erich. *Mimesis: The Representation of Reality in Western Literature.* Princeton, NJ: Princeton University Press, 2003.

Barnett, James H., and Rhoda Gruen. "Recent American divorce novels, 1938–1945: A study in the sociology of literature." *Social Forces* 26, no. 3 (1948): 322–327.

Bel, Jacqueline, and Thomas Vaessens, eds. *Women's Writing from the Low Countries 1880–2010: An Anthology.* Amsterdam: Amsterdam University Press, 2010.

Berelson, B., and P. Salter. "Majority and minority Americans: An analysis of magazine fiction." *Public Opinion Quarterly* 10, no. 2 (1946): 168–190.

Boven, Erica Maria Angela. *Een hoofdstuk apart: "Vrouwenromans" in de literaire kritiek 1898–1930.* Amsterdam: Sara/Van Gennep, 1992.

Brems, Hugo. *Altijd weer vogels die nesten beginnen: geschiedenis van de Nederlandse literatuur, 1945–2005.* Rotterdam: B. Bakker, 2006.

Briggs, X. "Ties that bind, bridge and constrain: Social capital and segregation in the American metropolis." In *Trabalho apresentado no International Seminar on Segregation and the City.* Cambridge: Lincoln Institute of Land Policy, 2001.

Chen, Yunsong, and Beate Volker. "Social capital and homophily both matter for labor market outcomes: Evidence from replication and extension." *Social Networks* 45 (2016): 18–31.

Collins, Patricia Hill. *Black Feminist Thought: Knowledge, Consciousness, and the Politics of Empowerment*. Abingdon: Routledge, 2008.

Culpeper, Jonathan. "A cognitive approach to characterization: Katherina in Shakespeare's *The Taming of the Shrew.*" *Language and Literature* 9, no. 4 (2000): 291–316.

Curtis, Neal, and Valentina Cardo. "Superheroes and third-wave feminism." *Feminist Media Studies* 18, no. 3 (2017): 381–396. DOI: 10.1080/14680777 .2017.1351387.

van der Deijl, L., Saskia Pieterse, Marion Prinse, and Roel Smeets. "Mapping the demographic landscape of characters in recent Dutch prose: A quantitative approach to literary representation." *Journal of Dutch Literature* 7, no. 1 (2016): 20–42.

Demeyer, Hans, and Sven Vitse. *Affectieve crisis, literair herstel: De romans van de millennialgeneratie*. Amsterdam: Amsterdam University Press, 2020.

Elson, D. K., N. Dames, and K. R. McKeown. "Extracting social networks from literary fiction." In *Proceedings of the 48th Annual Meeting of the Association for Computational Linguistics*, pp. 138–147. Uppsala: 2010.

English, James F. "Everywhere and nowhere: The sociology of literature after 'the sociology of literature.'" *New Literary History* 41, no. 2 (2010): v–xxiii.

Felski, Rita. *The Limits of Critique*. Chicago, IL: University of Chicago Press, 2015.

Freeman, Linton C. "Centrality in social networks conceptual clarification." *Social Networks* 1, no. 3 (1978): 215–239.

Freeman, Linton C. "The development of social network analysis." *A Study in the Sociology of Science* 1, no. 687 (2004): 159–167.

Frow, John. *Character and Person*. Oxford: Oxford University Press, 2014.

Fumaroli, Marc. "Houellebecq: baromètre social [Houellebecq: Social barometer]." *Le Point* (August 18, 2005): 63.

Gebauer, G. and Christoph Wulf. *Mimesis: Culture, Art, Society*. Translated by Don Reneau. Berkeley: University of California Press, 1995.

Glenn, Susan A. *Female Spectacle: The Theatrical Roots of Modern Feminism*. Cambridge, MA: Harvard University Press, 2002.

Govindan, V. K., and A. P. Shivaprasad. "Character recognition – a review." *Pattern Recognition* 23, no. 7 (1990): 671–683.

Granovetter, Mark S. "The strength of weak ties." *American Journal of Sociology* 78, no. 6 (1973): 1360–1380.

Grayson, S., K. Wade, G. Meaney, and D. Greene. "The sense and sensibility of different sliding windows in constructing co-occurrence networks from literature." In B. Bozic, G. Mendel-Gleason, C. Debruyne, and D. O'Sullivan D. (eds.), *Computational History and Data-Driven Humanities*. IFIP

Advances in Information and Communication Technology, vol. 482. Cham: Springer, 2016. https://doi.org/10.1007/978-3-319-46224-0_7.

Greenblatt, Stephen. *The Greenblatt Reader.* Hoboken, NJ: Wiley-Blackwell, 2005.

Greene, Gayle. *Changing the Story: Feminist Fiction and the Tradition.* Bloomington: Indiana University Press, 1991.

Gregory, Tobias. "Don't break that fiddle." *London Review of Books* 42, no. 22 (2020): 27.

Hansen, Derek L., Ben Shneiderman, Marc A. Smith, and B. Hogan. *Analyzing Social Media Networks with NodeXL.* Amsterdam: Elsevier, 2011.

Harari, Yuval Noah. *Sapiens: A Brief History of Humankind.* New York: Vintage Books, 2011.

Horkheimer, M., & T. W. Adorno. "The culture industry: Enlightenment as mass deception." In *Karl Marx* (pp. 405–424). Abingdon: Routledge, 2017.

Hunt, Lynn. *Inventing Human Rights: A History.* New York: Norton, 2007.

Inglis, Ruth A. "An objective approach to the relationship between fiction and society." *American Sociological Review* 3, no. 4 (1938): 526–533.

Jannidis, F. "Character." In P. Hühn et al. (eds.), *The Living Handbook of Narratology.* Berlin: De Gruyter, 2013. Retrieved from www.lhn.uni-ham burg.de/article/character.

Jayannavar, P., A. Agarwal, M. Ju, and O. Rambow. "Validating literary theories using automatic social network extraction." *Proceedings of NAACL-HLT Fourth Workshop of Computational Linguistics for Literature* (2015): 32–41. https://doi.org/10.3115/v1/w15-0704.

Karsdorp, F. B., Mike Kestemont, Christof Schöch, and Antal P. J. van den Bosch. "The love equation: Computational modeling of romantic relation-ships in French classical drama." *6th Workshop on Computational Models of Narrative (CMN '15)* (2015): 98–107.

Kelly, Adam. "David Foster Wallace and the new sincerity in American fiction." In David Hering (ed.), *Consider David Foster Wallace: Critical Essays*, pp. 131–146. Austin, TX: SSMG Press, 2010.

Kennedy, James. *Nieuw Babylon in aanbouw: Nederland in de jaren zestig.* Amsterdam: Boom, 1995.

Koolen, Corina. Reading beyond the female: The relationship between percep-tion of author gender and literary quality. Doctoral dissertation, Amsterdam University, 2018.

Kraicer, E., and Andrew Piper. "Social characters: The hierarchy of gender in contemporary English-language fiction." *Journal of Cultural Analytics* 1, no. 1 (2019): 1–28. https://doi.org/10.31235/osf.io/4kwrg.

Labatut, V. and Xavier Bost. "Extraction and analysis of fictional character networks: A survey." *ACM Computing Surveys* 52, no.5 (2019): 89. https://doi.org/10.1145/3344548.

Laughlin, K., J. Gallagher, D. Cobble, E. Boris, P. Nadasen, S. Gilmore, and L. Zarnow. "Is it time to jump ship? Historians rethink the waves metaphor." *Feminist Formations* 22, no. 1 (2010): 76–135. Retrieved June 22, 2021, from www.jstor.org/stable/40835345.

Lee, J. S., and C. Y. Yeung. "Extracting networks of people and places from literary texts." *Proceedings of the 26th Pacific Asia Conference on Language, Information, and Computation* (2012): 209–218.

Lee, J. S., and T. S. Wong. "Hierarchy of characters in the Chinese Buddhist canon." *Proceedings of the Twenty-Ninth International Florida Artificial Intelligence Research Society Conference* (2016).

Levine, Caroline. *Forms*. Princeton, NJ: Princeton University Press, 2015.

Lynch, Teresa, Jessica E. Tompkins, Irene I. van Driel, and Niki Fritz. "Sexy, strong, and secondary: A content analysis of female characters in video games across 31 years." *Journal of Communication* 66, no. 4 (August 2016): 564–584. https://doi.org/10.1111/jcom.12237.

Mann, Susan Archer, and Douglas J. Huffman. "The decentering of second-wave feminism and the rise of the third wave." *Science and Society* 69, no. 1 (2005): 56–91.

Marsden, P. V. "Core discussion networks of Americans." *American Sociological Review* 52 (1987): 122–313.

Marsden, P. V. "Homogeneity in confiding relations." *Social Networks* 10 (1988): 57–76.

McEaston, M. C. 2016. https://mceaston.com/2016/01/23/the-western-literary-canon-or-the-curious-case-of-the-male-ego/.

Meijer, Maaike. "Feminisme als taalstrijd. Reflecties over identiteit en subjectiviteit van vrouwen." *Taal en identiteit: Afrikaans en Nederlands: voordragte gehou in die Pieterskerk, Leiden 23–24 junie 1992 onder beskerming van die Afrika Studiecentrum/byeengebr. en ingel. deur Vernon February* (1994): 90–105.

Meijer, Maaike. *Machtige melodieën: Populaire teksten uit de jaren vijftig en zestig als bron voor cultuurgeschiedenis*. Inaugural lecture. Maastricht: Maastricht University, 1995.

Milgram, Stanley. "The small-world problem." *Psychology Today* 1, no. 1 (1967): 61–67.

Moi, Toril. "Rethinking character." In T. Moi, R. Felski, and A. Anderson (eds.), *Character: Three Inquiries in Literary Studies*, pp. 27–76. Chicago, IL: University of Chicago Press, 2020.

Moraru, Christian. *Cosmodernism: American Narrative, Late Globalization, and the New Cultural Imaginary.* Ann Arbor: University of Michigan Press, 2011.

Moravec, M., and K. K. Chang. "Feminist bestsellers: A digital history of 1970s feminism." *Journal of Cultural Analytics* 1, no. 1 (2021): 22333.

Moretti, Franco. "Network Theory, plot analysis." *Literary Lab Pamphlet 2* (May 1, 2011). https://litlab.stanford.edu/LiteraryLabPamphlet2.pdf.

Moretti, Franco. "Network Theory, plot analysis". *New Left Review* 68 (2011). https://newleftreview.org/issues/ii68/articles/franco-moretti-network-theory-plot-analysis.

Moretti, Franco. *Distant Reading.* London: Verso, 2013.

Philip Oltermann, "'At first I thought, this is crazy': The real-life plan to use novels to predict the next war." *The Guardian*, June 26, 2021. www.theguardian.com/lifeandstyle/2021/jun/26/project-cassandra-plan-to-use-novels-to-predict-next-war.

Pennell, H., and E. Behm-Morawitz. "The empowering (super) heroine? The effects of sexualized female characters in superhero films on women." *Sex Roles* 72 (2015): 211–220. https://doi.org/10.1007/s11199-015-0455-3.

Petersen, Rasmus. *Criminal Network Investigation: Processes, Tools, and Techniques.* PhD thesis. University of Southern Denmark (2012).

Potolsky, Matthew. *Mimesis.* The New Critical Idiom. Oxfordshire: Routledge, 2006.

Reicher, M. E. "The ontology of fictional character." In J. Eder, F. Jannidis, and R. Schneider (eds.), *Characters in Fictional Worlds: Understanding Imaginary Beings in Literature, Film, and Other Media*, pp.111–133. Berlin: de Gruyter, 2010.

Righart, Hans. *De eindeloze jaren zestig: Geschiedenis van een generatieconflict.* Amsterdam: De Arbeiderspers, 1995.

Schaub, Melissa. *Middlebrow Feminism in Classic British Detective Fiction: The Female Gentleman.* New York: Springer, 2013.

Shannon, E. A. The influence of feminism on public policy abortion and equal pay in Australia and the Republic of Ireland. Doctoral dissertation, University of Tasmania, 1997.

Showalter, Elaine. *A Literature of Their Own: British Women Novelists from Bronte to Lessing.* Princeton, NJ: Princeton University Press, 1977.

Showalter, Elaine. *A Jury of Her Peers: American Women Writers from Anne Bradstreet to Annie Proulx.* London: Virago Press, 2009.

Smeets, Roel, E. Sanders, and A. van den Bosch. "Character centrality in present-day Dutch literary fiction." *Digital Humanities Benelux Journal* 1 (2019): 71–90.

Smeets, Roel. *Character Constellations: Representations of Social Groups in Present-Day Dutch Literary Fiction*. Leuven: Leuven University Press, 2021.

Spivak, Gayatri. *The Post-Colonial Critic: Interviews, Strategies, Dialogues*. London: Routledge, 1990.

Stiller, J., D. Nettle, and R. I. M. Dunbar. "The small world of Shakespeare's plays." *Human Nature* 14, no. 4 (2003): 397–408.

Underwood, Ted. *Distant Horizons: Digital Evidence and Literary Change*. Chicago, IL: University of Chicago Press, 2019.

Underwood, Ted, David Bamman, and Sabrina Lee. "The transformation of gender in English-language fiction." *Cultural Analytics* (February 13, 2018). DOI:10.22148/16.019.

Van Boven, Erica. "De middlebrow-roman schrijft terug. Visies op elite en 'hoge literatuur' in enkele publieksromans rond 1930." *Tijdschrift voor Nederlandse Taal-en Letterkunde* 125, no. 3 (2011): 285–305.

Van Dijk, Yra, and Merlijn Olnon (2015). www.de-gids.nl/artikelen/radicaal-relationisme.

Volker, Beate, and Roel Smeets. "Imagined social structures: Mirrors or alternatives? A comparison between networks of characters in contemporary Dutch literature and networks of the population in the Netherlands." *Poetics* 79 (2019): 101379.

Vos, Leentje Cornelia. Uitzondering op de regel: De positie van vrouwelijke auteurs in het naoorlogse Nederlandse literaire veld. Doctoral dissertation, University of Groningen, 2008.

Watt, Ian. *The Rise of the Novel: Studies in Defoe, Richardson and Fielding*. Berkeley: University of California Press, 1960.

Wilde, Oscar. "The Decay of Lying – An Observation." In *Intentions*, 1891.

Digital Literary Studies

Katherine Bode
Australian National University

Katherine Bode is Professor of Literary and Textual Studies at the Australian National University. Her research explores the critical potential and limitations of computational approaches to literature, in publications including *A World of Fiction: Digital Collections and the Future of Literary History* (2018), *Advancing Digital Humanities: Research, Methods, Theories* (2014), *Reading by Numbers: Recalibrating the Literary Field* (2012), and *Resourceful Reading: The New Empiricism, eResearch and Australian Literary Culture* (2009).

Adam Hammond
University of Toronto

Adam Hammond is Assistant Professor of English at the University of Toronto. He is author of *Literature in the Digital Age* (Cambridge 2016) and co-author of *Modernism: Keywords* (2014). He works on modernism, digital narrative, and computational approaches to literary style. He is editor of the forthcoming *Cambridge Companion to Literature in the Digital Age* and *Cambridge Critical Concepts: Literature and Technology*.

Gabriel Hankins
Clemson University

Gabriel Hankins is Associate Professor of English at Clemson University. His first book is *Interwar Modernism and the Liberal World Order* (Cambridge 2019). He writes on modernism, digital humanities, and color. He is technical manager for the Twentieth Century Literary Letters Project and co-editor on *The Digital Futures of Graduate Study in the Humanities* (in progress).

Advisory Board

About the Series

Our series provides short exemplary texts that address a pressing research question of clear scholarly interest within a defined area of literary studies, clearly articulate the method used to address the question, and demonstrate the literary insights achieved.

Cambridge Elements ≡

Digital Literary Studies

Printed in the United States
by Baker & Taylor Publisher Services